WHAT PEOPLE AR

TEEN SPIRI
TO MODERN S\

Teen Spirit Guide to Modern Shamanism is a brilliant book! Kelley Harrell provides you with a wealth of tools to assist you in cultivating your own shamanic path. This is an important book to help readers create a life filled with depth and meaning. Great guide!
Sandra Ingerman, MA, author of *Soul Retrieval* and *Shamanic Journeying: A Beginner Guide*

Teen Spirit Guide to Modern Shamanism is fuel for both the head and the heart, offering young spiritual seekers grounded advice and experiential practices for exploring the path of modern shamanism.
Hillary S. Webb, Ph.D., author of *Exploring Shamanism, Traveling Between the Worlds: Conversations with Contemporary Shamans*, and *Yanantin and Masintin in the Andean World: Complementary Dualism in Modern Peru*

Long before the repression of shamanic vestiges in the witchcraft persecutions, the Western world lost its shamanic roots and the vital traditions that guided neophytes into this incredible world of the powers of nature. Without guidance for generations, our spiritual potentials have languished or worse, fallen prey to false gods and addictions. Yet the inherent potentials of shamanism still lie within us, and for those particularly gifted or called, these potentials still blossom as they have with Kelley Harrell. Her book presents her discoveries of how to approach our ancient potentials and provides guidance for those who find the shamanic path opening for them. While the neophyte shaman often walks a solitary path into the world of the spirits, the protection of the wisdom of our elders has always been essential guidance. Knowledge and experience from the wounded healers of the past can help those who walk the path today. Kelley's book provides guidance and wisdom to help structure the modern encounter with these ancient spiritual healing principles.

Dr. Michael Winkelman, M.P.H., Ph.D. Author of *Shamanism A Biopsychosocial Paradigm of Consciousness and Healing*

Teen Spirit Guide
to Modern
Shamanism

Teen Spirit Guide to Modern Shamanism

S. Kelley Harrell

Winchester, UK
Washington, USA

First published by Soul Rocks Books, 2014
Soul Rocks Books is an imprint of John Hunt Publishing Ltd., Laurel House, Station Approach,
Alresford, Hants, SO24 9JH, UK
office1@jhpbooks.net
www.johnhuntpublishing.com
www.soulrocks-books.com

For distributor details and how to order please visit the 'Ordering' section on our website.

Text copyright: S. Kelley Harrell 2013

ISBN: 978 1 78279 433 2

A CIP catalogue record for this book is available from the British Library.

Design: Stuart Davies
www.stuartdaviesart.com

Printed and bound by CPI Group (UK) Ltd, Croydon, CR0 4YY

We operate a distinctive and ethical publishing philosophy in all
areas of our business, from our global network of authors to
production and worldwide distribution.

To Maya and Tristan, to all of our wise young, for their courage to keep reminding us.

Acknowledgements

Thank you to Hillary S. Webb for her graceful contribution to this book, and for her fearlessness in affirming modern shamanism through her own work.

I'm grateful for the path that found me, and for the work and sacrifice of so many who enable it to move forward, still.

Thank you to dear Rob, for believing in my wild.

Thanks to my editor, Dominic James, for smoothing the wrinkles.

Many thanks to Publisher, Alice Grist, for planting the seeds to see what's right in front of me differently.

Foreword

In a way, I had it made, growing up where I did. Salem, Massachusetts—the historical site of the 1692-93 witch trials, and a place which in recent years had become a kind of Mecca for those interested in exploring the weird and the wyrd. In those days, it was not unusual to see someone walking down the street wearing a black cape or cloak, often with a pendant of the crescent moon slung around his or her neck. Esoteric bookstores and herbal apothecaries lined the streets; palm and tarot readers sat at small, cloth-covered tables on the sidewalks. Back then, Laurie Cabot, the "Official Witch of Salem," was often in the papers, always up to some kind of benign but newsworthy shenanigans.

I don't know if growing up in that environment was responsible for my childhood passion for exploring the reality-beyond-reality or if it was something that I was born with. Either way, living in Salem allowed me to immerse myself in such phenomena as clairvoyance, astral projection, lucid dreaming, energy healing, and so many other ways of knowing that our society tells us aren't real. I had no mentor to guide me. I was a shy eleven-year-old and afraid to ask for help. I was afraid to talk to my parents about my interests, for fear that they would think I was weird, or crazy, or—much, much worse—that they would make me stop. And so I went on alone.

I can't remember exactly what set me off, but at some point I was suddenly overcome with the fear that exploring non-ordinary reality in this way—alone, without guidance—might lead me to lose touch with ordinary reality. With that, I tossed out all my books and potions and shut that passion away. More than a decade later, while in my mid-twenties, I was introduced to modern shamanism. And on this spiritual and psychological path I found exactly what I had been looking for all those years ago. I had found a set of tools and techniques for entering into non-ordinary states of awareness in which I could access tangible, useable knowledge—about myself, about the world around me—in a way that defies our current scientific models of how such knowing is attained. It was a way of interacting with the world that jived with some deeply buried part of me. Just as importantly, I had found a group of teachers and a community with whom I could share the profound experiences that followed.[1] With that, my early passion was reignited and thus became a directing force within my personal and professional life.

I wish I'd had *Teen Spirit Guide to Modern Shamanism* back in those early days, when I was young and just starting out. If you've picked up (or downloaded) this book, it's probably because, like so many of us, you feel an irresistible pull towards non-ordinary realms of experience. If so, you have come to the right place. Kelley Harrell, herself a long-time, committed seeker, recognizes your passion and, within the pages that follow, offers wise guidance to assist you in cultivating your own personalized shamanic path; teaching you how to access the stories and gifts that are uniquely yours and then put them to good use within daily life.

To discover these stories and gifts is no easy task for, as one of my shamanic teachers says, "The farthest we'll ever have to travel is from our heads to our hearts."[2] There are many twists and turns on the path from the head to the heart; many stops and starts and, very often, more questions than answers. But times have changed since I was a teen. As Harrell writes so eloquently and encouragingly in the first few pages, "We don't have to do it alone anymore."

Thank goodness for that. *Teen Spirit Guide to Modern Shamanism* is fuel for both the head and the heart, offering young spiritual seekers grounded advice and experiential practices for exploring the path of modern shamanism.

Hillary S. Webb, PhD.

Author, *Yanantin and Masintin in the Andean World: Complementary Dualism in Modern Peru; Exploring Shamanism;* and *Traveling Between the Worlds: Conversations with Contemporary Shamans*

Maine

2013

Preface

The sun, moon, and the stars are our first awareness that something greater than ourselves exists. To us they are timeless, permanent. Fixed points guiding our shifting consciousness, having witnessed the creation of Earth and evolution of humanity, they shape our awareness of how we relate to every living thing. With their infinite perspective, if you could engage them and know their wisdom, their origin, their destiny, would you?

That's animism. Considered the oldest religion, it's an ancient expression of awareness beyond the self. Through dreams and trance states, this spark once lit every major world religion. The belief that everything has a soul, all souls are connected thus can intercommunicate, and that all souls are equal is a potent vantage point on a humbling path.

Now imagine being able to talk with the spirit of anything in life, better yet—All That Is. What dialogue could emerge between you and a blade of grass? How might learning the spiritual plight of an aeons-extinct ethnic group enrich your life choices? Hearing the voice of living space, would you inhabit it differently?

This is shamanism: the practice of communicating with the soul in All Things. When I say 'practice' I don't mean repeating an act until you get it right. In this use, it means to instill regular discipline to accomplish a specific task, ritual without which we feel incomplete, or that our experience of each day is less.

Shamanism is an expression of animism. Everything that is alive is alive, so the sages say, and if we allow ourselves to engage in that openness, how we create our radiant selves and manifest wild lives can be radically transformed forever.

In modern terms, what does this mean? If you can risk being

4

the crazy person talking to yourself, there may be a shaman in you, yet.

Dream well,

~skh

2013

Our Wise Young

In Western culture it's an oxymoron to suggest that young people are wise, that they could provide informed counsel amongst themselves or to adults. Yet we romanticize childhood as a primal connection to Source, intuition that weakens the more we seat into form, society, adulthood. In reality, children arrive animists. They learn about life, themselves, and empathy by imagining the liveliness of everything they come into contact with. Yet abandoning such child's play is a hallmark of maturation in the West. Such contradiction has closed our eyes to the value the young bring to our cultural spiritual path.

Likewise, most of us aren't raised in spiritual traditions that support our juicy knowing. Many have been forced to suppress intuition and abilities, useful life skills that happen not to be honored in our culture.

Not having a connection to a particular tradition doesn't preclude being able to choose a shamanic path. It doesn't mean that you can't still cultivate extraordinary abilities in a way that is quite practical, if not helpful. In fact, know that seeking to know more about shamanism indicates firm trust in inner guidance. Despite its prominence now, you don't stumble onto the path of shamanism. That odd trail blazes itself to you.

In my childhood I was aware that I experienced phenomena those around me did not. I saw spirits of both the deceased and the living, I had prophetic dreams, I could sense and sometimes see life force, and I was aware of aspects of my soul leaving and returning. Of course I wasn't raised with a vocabulary for what any of this was, let alone the awareness that having these experiences was not just okay, but natural. Having been raised in a traditional path of organized religion, I didn't decide to explore my abilities until I was seventeen years old. In fact, it didn't occur to me until then that my innate abilities could be considered skills that I could hone and use.

Given that context, I'm a pretty standard Caucasian, middle-class American woman. I have some interesting genealogy that could comprise indigenous spiritual whisperings that may have echoed softly through the animistic perspective of my grand-father. But I wasn't raised in such teachings. I am from what is considered in modern shamanism a "broken path," meaning, my ancestors may have been Celts and Eastern Cherokee, but I wasn't raised in those traditions, myself. Through the hardship of seeking mysticism in a culture that denounces it and my own insatiable desire to create myself as I truly feel I am, I chose to return to traditions that supersede ancestry.

I came into my abilities as a child, and to shamanism as my personal path in young adulthood. I began working with others as a modern shaman in 1998, and established my practice, Soul Intent Arts, in 2000. To see my path so succinctly summarized in two sentences doesn't give proper credence to how hard it was to find resources on shamanism in the 1980s-90s, or how alone I was in the creation of a modern shamanic presence in the suburban southeastern United States. It isn't that way now, and part of my professional practice has been to establish the Tribe of the Modern Mystic, to create community for others who feel isolated in the realization of spiritual awareness. Still, even in woo woo circles, shamanism is the fringe of the fringe. It's widely misunderstood and characterized by gender, ethnic, and psycho-logical bias, as well as superstition.

We don't have to wear animal skins, shake bird vertebra, and speak in tongues to be shamans, though we can if we want to. Spirit Guides will visit us if we wear Ugg boots and jeans just as easily. Specific training and classes aren't required to lead a shamanic life, or even to become a shaman. Indeed, we are all shamanic in nature, though we have not all accepted the role of shaman. I draw a marked distinction between the two, as one who holds a shamanic life view for self, and one who assumes the role of working with others as a shaman. Regardless of what initiation is received, I suggest intensely studying shamanism, and suspect the deeper you travel into the spirit realm so directly, a desire blossoms to learn how to do so better, with someone who understands the ropes, as well as how they can ensnare.

Having a mentor is critical in learning shamanism in a safe, grounded practice. I know that's very 'pot/kettle.' I didn't have a mentor, yet I insist it's a must. The thing is, when I was seeking, there weren't mentors. I remained self-taught for a decade before I found someone who could help me shape my work. Now, there are those who not only model animistic life, but share their wisdom openly. We don't have to do it alone and stumbling anymore. As well, many great articles and books are available to learn the bare bones of shamanism, also online and in-person classes offered around the world. Raw talent and basic skills aside, I wholeheartedly encourage finding someone to be co-accountable in the process of learning to navigate the world of the wyrd, and how to healthily set the boundaries in soul work.

Learning shamanism isn't just about acquiring techniques in how to do it, but also how to incorporate and deal with the changes it brings to everyday life. A weekend class can teach how to go into the spirit world in a more informed way, though it can't impart what to do with the information gained from it, or how to process it into a changed perspective that works.

For that reason, throughout reading this book, begin searching for a shaman to work with. Feel free to contact me to help find someone nearby. The information here will facilitate arrival to a mentor more informed, aware of the challenges that may rise, and with a clearer sense of why shamanism now.

What do you think?

Consider your options for widening your shamanic education. You are the best person to gauge how you learn. Do you thrive in self-paced studies, or do you need a group to bounce off of? Do you need weekly accountability, or is daily more your speed? Can you learn in isolation, or do you need regular face time? What qualities do you need most in a teacher? In studies?

The great thing about learning an esoteric skill is that you get to craft your approach to learning it, and you can in large part do it your way. Be honest with yourself about how you learn best, your willingness to set aside daily time to devote to your studies, and go for it with your heart singing!

Part I – What Shamans Are

The History of Shamanism

Talking about shamanism without dabbling a bit into history is like trying to drive a Bentley with no engine. I'll keep it as brief and light as possible, though this is definitely a case of knowing what you're coming from to create where you're going.

No one knows when exactly animism, thus shamanism, began. Noted scholars on archaic religious roots, such as Michael Ripinsky-Naxon and Robert Wallis, approach it as a natural development of human awareness, an emergence of expression from shared emotions, empathy, and dreams, resulting in a desire to find meaning in them.[3]

Early researchers of shamanism studied indigenous tribes and ancient artifacts for information on ecstatic religious rituals. Most prominent among these is historian Mircea Eliade, and his groundbreaking tome of the 1950s, *Shamanism: Archaic Techniques of Ecstasy*. Eliade's work set the tone for how shamanism would be accepted in the modern world, shedding light onto a little-known path, while creating biases and erroneous assumptions that exist, still. For example, in his world study of various shamanistic cultures, he deduced that none honored women as true shamans, which having expanded our worldly knowledge, we now accept as not true[4]. The oldest skeletal remains of a shaman belonged to a woman.[5] Female shamans were present throughout history in many cultures, including Chile, Siberia, and China. As well, he didn't address sexual orientation, specifically a pervasive concept that shamans walk between worlds, and also stand between gender. Thus, through decades of study after his omission, the role of women and queer sexuality in shamanism was disregarded.

Without question, the man responsible for bringing

shamanism into modern awareness is Michael Harner, author of *The Way of the Shaman*. Not without its biases and accusations of cultural appropriation, Harner's work presented what he considered a cultureless approach to shamanic technique, which he called "Core Shamanism." He went on to found The Foundation for Shamanic Studies, which has in many ways branded shamanism around the world.

Some of our best insight into the human experience of the unseen most recently has been in the work of anthropologist Michael Winkelman, specifically, *Shamanism – a Biopsychosocial Paradigm of Consciousness and Healing*. By linking base human neurological function to the work of Jung and others focused on common human ecstatic experience, as well as to base motor function, valuable insight into not just "why" shamanism, but "how" shamanism is clarified.

You can see that for the most part, in Western discussion, shamanism has been dominated by academics, based in anthro-pology, and most recently psychologists and ethnographers, with their own cultural, ethnic, social, and psychological biases. Accounts of animistic societies and how shamanism thrummed through daily life were not valued; thus, they weren't made available in the 'civilized world.' Until the last decade, there were no personal accounts of contemporary people using these ancient techniques, an omission that served as motivation to write my memoir, *Gift of the Dreamtime*.

Given our scholarly yet rocky acceptance of shamanism, there is a tendency in the West to believe that shamanism is Native American. In reality, most Native Americans never heard the word "shaman" until it became popular in modern use, and to refer to a Native American tribal spiritual leader as such—and possibly that of other cultures—is insulting. A broader truth is that some animistic perspective and mystical expression of that awareness pervaded every culture. What we call that and how we describe the details is still under scrutiny.

With the question of the origin of shamanism in mind, we do know the origin of the term. It would be remiss of me not to mention that in wider circles, many consider the term 'shaman' hijacked from the Tungus Evinki tribe. Originating from the word šamán, a form of the Chinese sha men, meaning "Buddhist monk," it is assumed to be derived from the Sanskrit word *sramana*, meaning "Buddhist ascetic."[6] Because of its geographic specificity, strict scholars say that 'shaman' refers to practitioners of a specific role, in Northern Asia. The idea that the word describes a general ecstatic interspiritual practice, or mystics from diverse cultures, is considered an insult. This specificity is something to keep in mind as you venture into various studies of shamanism, as well as the diverse personalities who shape it.

Along with disputes over the title, there are concerns around the cultural appropriation of various components of shamanism. I mentioned earlier, most of us who are descended from Western European roots (and other cultural groups) are on a broken path, spiritually speaking. Somewhere in our past branches an enormous family tree, comprised of all sorts of animistic, pre-Abrahamic roots. Most of us would have to go pretty far back to trace such a tradition to the present, and only for a small minority is that even possible. The rest of us respond to a cellular calling, perhaps intellectual or heart-centered interest in older paths, and find ourselves making peace with a lot of misconceptions, challenged personal truths, and frayed religious ends. Others of us hold spiritual interests with no ties to our genetic heritage. Some calling beyond DNA or upbringing leads us beyond convention into a world view and spiritual discipline far outside our familiar.

Whatever the reason, in the social global community, many now explore spiritual approaches not native to the home hearth. Some see this expansion as a positive expression, crossing inter-cultural barriers and widening awareness. Others see it as a right, possibly a destiny or obligation. However we feel about delving into the spiritual traditions of another culture, keep in mind how the influence of outsiders impacts that tradition and its greater culture.

Sadly, cultural appropriation is a problem because historically non-natives have sought to participate in, use, claim, and/or profit from native practices. Poaching rituals, garb, and even cosmologies then presented as original creations have plagued the modern shamanic movement. Other injustices come in the form of judgments against indigenous practitioners, sending the message that they are savages. Pervasive still are the ideas that shamanistic tribes lack a civilized worldview, that paganism and other earth-based religions clash with Western Abrahamic philosophies, that the use of entheogens (psychoactive substances) to induce trance states is required, that shamanism can only be dark sorcery, and the incessant questioning of the mental stability of practitioners.

A racist notion found in neoshamanic circles is placing high value on indigenous wisdom but not on indigenous people. Spiritual tourism, or adventuring to remote locations to find enlightenment, has by and large ignored that while the numbers of neoshamans increase, the number of indigenous shamans (and their tribes) decrease, a hypocritical gesture that perpetuates the idea of the noble savage. [7]

There are many factors to consider when approaching the customs of a culture of which one doesn't originate. I don't wish to impress that it's wrong to venture into another culture's wisdom. Rather, carefully consider the reasons for doing so, how our presence in this tradition changes it, and how we can honor the cultural differences in our own practice. The bottom line is, the question of who gets to be a shaman has been asked for centuries, and it continues to be asked, even now.

What do you think?

What strikes you most about the history of shamanism? How does its history impact its modern practice? What influence does cultural sensitivity have on modern practice? Does learning about the history of shamanism stir cellular memories for you?

Consider how you might celebrate the rituals of a group of which you are not native. How might you show respect for such rituals? How does your culture influence your spiritual path? Your biogender and sexual orientation?

Take time to sit with intuitive, intellectual, and sensual reactions that rise as you connect with the past of shamanism, its various cultural considerations, and where you would like to go along your shamanic path.

The Religion of Ecstasy

I'm not the academic to elaborate on whether shamanism is a religion, though I offer many resources throughout this book from scholars who are, and hope to provoke catharsis to shape personal conclusions. While its religio-philosophic status may not be widely relevant to all, how we view religion consciously or unconsciously shapes our shamanic path.

Many consider shamanism the root of all religions, the hardwired neurological ecstatic experience of awe that every human has, no matter what belief system we identify with. It is perhaps best described as the mystic component or practice of many religions, though it isn't the religion-proper. While it doesn't have set doctrines or a presiding court, our base motor function asserts common experiences, not just across culture, but throughout recorded history. Likewise, a lot of people view it as a life perspective free of rules and doctrine, ready to be experienced by anyone who wants to go on the adventure and explore uncharted lands.

Ecstasy? In this use, the term refers to a trance state in which normal consciousness is transcended, possibly with the experiences of visions, visitations by spirits, or some knowing of expanded consciousness. Where animism may be considered a life perspective, shamanism is a way to experience and express that perspective. While there is a widely accepted framework for how to do that, the beauty of shamanism is there are no set rules.

I first learned of shamanism in junior high World Cultures class, like most everyone else in my generation. I thought it was a thing of the past, or done only by people in faraway exotic places. The summer that I turned seventeen, several wyrd factors collided, ensuring that shamanism was alive and well. First, after a prophetic collision of two queen bees, my family experienced the unexpected deaths of two elders exactly one month apart;

then I read a modern account of shamanism that left me stunned.

The story I read was of a chronically depressed woman who went to visit a Native American spirit healer. The man did a soul retrieval for her, and as the woman described the process, I knew before reading each paragraph what would happen next. I understood the steps of soul retrieval without ever having read or been told about it. That moment defined my relationship to shamanism forever, sealing the fate between my freaky childhood experiences and young adult paranormal adventures. Shamanism wasn't a thing of the past. It was in the present, and had always been.

Early on my path, I was quick to assert that shamanism is not a religion. The association smacked too much of a path I wanted to leave behind, and of a belief system that confined me. Now, many years and a lot of experience later, I'm not as quick to detract. While I personally don't approach it as such, I respect that many traditional shamans do. I can easily see how the menagerie of totems and guides one has inherited or amassed, the relationships formed with elements, stones, places, and souls, and the discipline required on a regular basis to maintain integrity in those bonds could be considered a personal or cultural religion.

Regardless of personal perspective, keep in mind that for many traditional shamans, it is a religious experience. If we all have to come to our unique understandings of what shamanism is, why does it matter what others think it is? Maybe it doesn't. My status as someone looking across the historic landscape of shamanism begs me to step out of my contemporary viewpoint and understand the historic, cultural, ethnic, and possibly racial biases of blatantly stating that shamanism is not a religion. As well, it reminds me that traditional shamans are likely not having this discussion at all. Only the modern mind needs it pinned down, which in itself is telling.

What do you think?

What components of religion are important to you? Which ones aren't?

How does shamanism differ from how you think of religion? Of a natural human function? Is it possible to view shamanism as both a spiritual experience and an innate function?

If you consider shamanism an innate function, do you think everyone has this ability?

Consider your comfort level in developing your inherent abilities with a disciplined study. Regardless of how freeform your approach to shamanism is, it will eventually require focused discipline. What feelings are stirred with the idea of bringing structured guidance to the center of your intimate temple?

Engaging Ecstasy

Shamanic journeying, also called ecstatic journeying, is the trance state we enter to visit the spirit world. Often journeying is erroneously called 'meditation' and 'guided visualization,' even pathworking. Certainly there are many ways to meditate, that may be considered shamanic. However, the practice of ecstatic journeying, the technique which distinguishes shamanism from all other intuitive arts, is very specific.

Meditation can be any collected approach to stilling the mind and generating relaxation. It may have a specific focus, or be completely open, and while not intended, often results in intense spiritual revelations. Likewise, guided visualization and pathworking are forms of directed meditation, in which participants are gently told how to move through the experience, what possibilities for relaxation and awareness (or totems and worlds) are available, and the actions that must be taken to achieve them.

Students first learning to journey are often instructed using specific inductions to aid their shift into trance. Once therein, what they do and how they experience that space is unique. Holding fast to the intention for the work, spirit travel is neither guided, nor nebulously left open. That said, journeying is actively engaging the spirit realm, at a very high level of self, for the sole purpose of learning insight into healing oneself, another, or a collective need. When that wisdom has been imparted and travel back to waking is completed, plans for how that insight can be manifest are implemented at once.

Having distinguished meditation from journeying, the ability to relax on command and to maintain mindfulness are invaluable skills to supplement ecstatic trance. The ability to ease into trance isn't always easy for some; thus, using mindfulness techniques can help with the flight out. Likewise, sometimes brilliant, mind-blowing information we learn in trance demands therein that we change some component of character or habit may not be comfortable to implement in our mundane lives. As we form relationships with inner and other worlds, as well as guides, our daily life often shifts in distressing ways. Falling back on a range of anti-stress techniques can facilitate every point of the journey to shamanhood.

Mindfulness techniques that I use and teach students to supplement their trance development are:

- The Buddhist practice of *Tonglen*
- The Huna ritual of Ho'o opono pono
- Holotropic breathwork
- Thought Field Therapy or Emotional Freedom Technique
- Reiki

What do you think?

Have you had experiences in which you felt not in your body? How did you know that you were out of your body? In what way did these experiences feel different than dreams or daydreams? How did you feel during these experiences?

Make a list of situations, spaces, sounds, sensations, thoughts, feelings, and memories that quiet you inside. When we are stilled within, we hold an openness that allows us to feel peaceful, yet grow into the quiet, itself. Take care to distinguish that which brings you comfort from what inspires stillness. While comfort may soothe, we tend to saturate in it so much that it becomes an emotional experience. When we become emotionally involved with the focus of our quiet, we're no longer in balance. By focusing solely on that which brings your inner and outer worlds into quiet peace, you honor the thing, the stillness you have created, and what can be created from it.

At least once a day, sit quietly and imagine one thing from your list of experiences that soothe you. Sit with it until it fills you so completely that you hear it, smell it, become it. As you increase the frequency and duration of this relationship to the things that ground you, you become more grounded throughout your daily routine.

Harrell

What Shamans Do

Called medicine men, wise women, skywalkers, nagual, spirit-walkers, and many more titles and roles, the purpose of the shaman is as diverse. Shamanism employs a method of interacting with the spirit world and with spirit helpers, which while in deep trance, the shaman wills an aspect of his or her soul to travel from the body to a specific destination in the spirit realm for the purpose of bringing back healing for an individual, a community, a place, the self, etc.

That's a mouthful, I know, yet each part of it not only elaborates on the role of the shaman, but delineates it from all other intuitive practices. It is this focused vehicle of soul travel that distinguishes shamanism from any other form of trance, mediumship, or healing work. Being a medium who can communicate with souls isn't the same as one who can interact with them. Such is the difference between listening in on a conversation and changing the subject.

In short, shamans deconstruct the accepted order to restore flow of power: take energy out that doesn't belong and put energy back that belongs. Roles a shaman may don to restore balance can include:

- **Medium** – communicating with diverse consciousness
- **Ritual and Ceremonialist** – crafting rituals and ceremonies for specific observations
- **Channeler** – bringing a consciousness into one's form
- **Excorcist** – removing a consciousness from one's form
- **Diviner** – gaining insight into a situation by using an oracle
- **Energy worker** – balancing life force/chi/prana
- **Herbologist** – working with plants as healing agents
- **Therapist** – pastoral caregiving to support physical,

emotional, mental and psychological needs

Many sum this list into a single word: healer. While some sit comfortably with this title regarding how they work with others, others find it very uncomfortable, if not inaccurate. I think of it as incomplete, as in my experience, no one heals us. No doctor, procedure, plant, spirit, or medicine heals us. We heal ourselves. I think of myself as someone who facilitates healing, thus am leery of practitioners of any modality who proclaim themselves to be healers. Not only does it claim ownership of the transaction, it creates an artificial hierarchy in which the client can never become empowered. Without that empowerment, healing can't "stick." In that light, there are differing comfort levels with the term, as well as what it indicates about a practitioner's ability.

Given the range of roles shamans use, it's important to understand how the skills they employ apply to everyday life. In the most broad perspective, shamans promote healing. Specific beliefs supporting how that healing is done are common across cultures of shamanism, such as:

- *Nature guides assist us.* Totems that may be plant, animal, element, mythic or extinct help us travel to the spirit worlds, as well as perform tasks there. The subsequent section *Totems* discusses Nature allies more in-depth.
- *Spirit, or angelic guides assist us.* Similar to totems, Spirit Guides help us meet our needs in the spirit worlds, and act as personal counsel on our path. The subsequent section *Spirit Guides* discusses spirit helpers more in-depth.
- *The soul is made up of infinite parts, which can become lost, thus retrieved.* Often when there is trauma, an aspect of the soul becomes distanced. I describe this state as "shelved," though common vernacular is "lost". It's natural for soul parts to travel in and out of our awareness, even without us knowing, as this exchange in the pool of All Things is one

way we expand our consciousness. In times of trauma, when a soul part leaves and can't return to the earthly consciousness, problems arise: chronic illness, feelings of depression, lack of motivation, feelings of not being completely present. Phrases such as "I'm beside myself," "I was frightened to pieces," "I feel lost," "I feel like part of me is missing," originate from a sense of soul loss. This is the point that a shaman is called to retrieve the soul part from the spirit realm, to heal it, then return it to All Things or to the individual.

- *Illness and/or undesirable behaviors can be removed from the etheric field.* In the trance state, imbalances are observed symbolically in the etheric field (the chakra system and bioenergetic layers that permeate and surround the form). By engaging and interacting with these symbols, life force can be balanced for healing.
- *Souls must be escorted to and from their physical forms, at birth and death.* Spiritual midwifing of a soul into form and death walking (psychopomp) a soul of the deceased back to Source are considered healthy practices not just for the individual, but for All Things.
- *Recognition of the connection of All Things.* Animism at its simplest. Understanding that an individual doesn't become ill, the whole community does, pervades shamanic cultures. Likewise, particular illnesses indicate imbalance in specific bioregions, communities, and families. Through treating the whole, the individual is healed. When an individual heals, wellness becomes contagious.

Beyond the basic functions a shaman performs and the framework of soul travel, the similarities across cultures largely stop there.

What do you think?

What experiences have you had that might be considered shamanic?

How do you feel about calling yourself a healer? What ego reactions do you have to that word? The idea?

As you create your relationship not only to shamanism as a practice, but as a role, consider what words seem accurate, appropriate, and affirming. List the words that describe your personal spiritual path, and words that describe how you manifest your role of shaman.

How can you shape your practice to support your relationship to shamanism? How can you create a dialogue to communicate it to others?

That's Crazy Talk

Delving deeply into discussion of shamanism eventually reveals correlations between mental illness and trance states. Specifically, for many people, the idea of talking to discarnate beings or inanimate objects is crazy.

Well, crazy is in the eye of the beholder.

Keep in mind that most of our studies on psychology and shamanism were done by Western white men observing tribal groups of other ethnicities. Specifically, they were anthropologists without backgrounds in mind/behavioral sciences and without sensitivity training. This bias has created disparate parallels that pervade assumptions about shamanism, like women who hear voices and express contact with spirits are seen as evil and ill, though men who experience the same phenomena are considered gifted intuitives. Because of the early perspectives put forward in academic publications regarding shamanism, negative connotations of shamans have been carried into modern mindsets. In Western culture intuitive gifts are frequently dismissed as outright pathology. This key predicament has been a stumbling block for many neoshamans.

Generally speaking, individuals exhibiting characteristics of mental conditions, such as bipolar swings and schizophrenia, in tribal settings are treated respectfully and are considered gifted mystics. In fact, people who speak in tongues, automatically slip into trance, channel spirits, etc., are considered valuable assets. This doesn't mean that the spiritual welfare of the community is wholly turned over to anyone with these characteristics. There is a process for determining that the individual can control going into and out of trance, as well as make informed choices while in trance, and root the wisdom of the journey in the daily needs of the tribe or individual. In this case, intuitive gifts are blessed, the tribal seer teaches the individual how to use his or her intuition, and the community supports the individual to assure his or her growth into shaman. Likewise, the realization that people who cannot control their trance experiences are not acting in a shamanic capacity, despite that they display intuitive ability, is respected and cared for accordingly. They are considered valuable intuitives, without the bestowal of the role of shaman.

Modern culture is neither as respectful, nor as accommodating to individuals having an experience of awe, whatever its origins. First off, we don't differentiate a psychotic experience from a spiritual one. Episodes of hearing voices, wide mood swings, and changes in overall personality are heavily medicated, treated through conventional models of psychiatric care, hospitalization, and medical intervention. Whatever the origins of their experiences, such individuals are all assessed with the same one-stop diagnoses, and are treated within the confines of closely monitored conventional care. There is no affirmation of the experience of awe through these mental challenges, no credence observed in how these individuals can benefit society, and no facilitation of the spiritual components of crisis to a mature and applicable life change.

One reaction to an archaic mental health system using outdated modalities is a social caricature of the shaman that has taken root in the New Age. The misunderstanding that traditional shamans treat the mentally ill with greater respect has fed a movement that negates the effectiveness of medical intervention. As a result, a push to use only alternative healing practices to treat mental illness has emerged. Part of this reaction has fed the romanticized idea that anyone having a psychotic episode is a shaman. Not only does this misinformation put undue pressure on the mentally ill and potentially label stable individuals as possible threats, it creates a dynamic in which serious underlying needs are not met. Fortunately, many mental health professionals are becoming educated to suss out spiritual emergency from true psychotic episodes, and to treat both from a holistic health model.[8] Despite that success, we have a long way to go before cultural perception or validation of such experiences occurs. In short, not all who have mental conditions are shamans, and not all shamans have mental conditions.

As the mental state of the shaman is questioned, often the legitimacy of illness in those seeking a shaman's help is scrutinized. Because the reasons that many seek the help of a shaman lie outside the bounds of Western cultural norms, thus the client lacks a vocabulary to articulate the concern, it takes a great deal of courage to venture along the path of shamanism, as the shaman or the client.

The Shaman's Death

Another idea to keep in mind while considering the psychological view of shamanism follows the animistic notion that all things are connected. While examining the connection of mental state to innate skill and shamanic role, consider that imbalance in an individual is not separate from imbalance in his or her collective or community. From this fundamental understanding, the base mechanic of shamanism is derived.

Psychological crisis is often the catalyst perceived as the calling to shamanism. Not all, but many shamans indicate having an experience that we now refer to as a spiritual emergency, a defining moment so profound that the way they view themselves and the world was permanently changed. Integrating that changed perspective in a community that rejects the change or doesn't understand it creates deep distress that may manifest psychological disturbances, or produce similar symptoms in the individual. The ability to move through this experience to an acceptance of the new world view is a hallmark of shamanism. This metamorphosis is referred to as a classic "shamanic death." Rising from such psychic hurt came the phrase "wounded healer," or someone who has survived intense pain by journeying into the wound, and in doing so, learned to thrive beyond it.

This timeless story of death and rebirth is known as the shamanic narrative, or more commonly, a healing story. Healing stories are magickal tales born from personal tribulation and victory, which are then shared. The process of sharing the personal narrative has several effects:

- In hearing the story, empathy is generated in listeners. They feel the emotions of the storyteller, which stir memories and feelings of their similar experience.
- Listeners become inspired. They own and value their personal stories.
- Listeners' personal stories are evoked. The wound is witnessed, thus healing becomes possible, as does a vision for life beyond the wound. Through ownership of the process healing occurs.
- Listeners tell their stories. Inspiration is shared.

Healing oneself is key to eventually working with others. The idea isn't that we become free of all affliction. Rather, we develop and commit to using the healing resources available to us. Through actively balancing the hardships of life, we gain insight into how better to be of service to others. We attract those who need the help and insight we have to give. We attract people who are or have gone through situations similar to our own.

There is no more animistic a mechanism than the healing story. Connection to and activation of the symbols in the story create the basic structure for shamanic healing. In this tradition of one person sharing the narrative, a single story heals a village.

A common discussion that arises in modern shamanic forums is the question of whether an initiatory wound is a requirement of shamanism. Certainly many contemporary seekers come to shamanism for self-healing. In fact, a criticism of modern shamanism is that many who come to it for that reason never evolve past personal need, never grow into the role, thus never emerge from the crisis as a shaman to assist others. In that light, traditional shamans do not consider such individuals true to the path. They are not seen as able to transmute their personal stories into a healing narrative functional for all.

What about those arriving on this course out of curiosity or an otherwise undefinable draw? Certainly, this scenario is more likely to take place in the modern context. Observing shamanism as a progressive path of personal healing and amassing of spiritual allies to facilitate healing in others, not having a healing need would seem to put one at a disadvantage in that process. Likewise, it would seemingly go against the spirit of healing, itself, to assume that everyone must have a wound in order to be empathetic or stand firmly as an active conduit of All Things.

My experience is that not everyone must have an initiatory wound to explore shamanism, though often in that exploration personal challenges arise that create dissonance with the current status quo. In other words, the way you live can't stay the same, once you've begun this process. Even wanted changes needed to sustain on the path can indeed incite deep distress. The path of shamanism once begun isn't shut down. Also, it doesn't stay neatly confined to specific life areas, or only when in trance. It becomes a lifestyle that demands expansion and acknowledgement through all facets of existence. In this way, the path becomes both the wound and the balm, echoing the recursive nature of both the wounded healer and the shamanic narrative.

What do you think?

How do you correlate mental illness with shamanism? What distinctions do you find in each?

Consider your biases around how men and women express intuition. Do you tend to see one as more intuitive than the other? Can you look within yourself and locate the source of that belief?

What is your healing story? Write it, and consider who might find inspiration from it.

Also, examine your thoughts around the idea of wounding. Is everyone wounded? What constitutes a wound? What indicates its healing? When does that process end?

How a Shaman is Called

We've talked about where shamans originated, what they do, and the general perception of them. Most curious is how someone becomes one. Traditionally they:

- Inherit the role
- Are called by the spirits
- Appoint themselves

Some might say there is an underlying call from the spirits in each of these options. Shamans who inherit the role still undergo training, though their ability to win approval of their community comes with a certain amount of automatic cred. Those spontaneously called may be visited by the tribal totem or may have a prophetic dream, the symbolism of which signals to the individual and the tribe the support of the spirits. Again, while training must be completed, a collective recognition is in place from the onset of selection. Traditional shamans generally view self-appointed shamans as having less power than those called by the spirits or inheriting the role, as there is no innate recognition of power in such individuals. While they may still be trained, these initiates have a tougher time proving their skills to their community. From that worldview, all modern shamans on broken paths would be considered lesser—which is to say, almost all of them.

I think the common experience is that modern shamans are called by the spirits; we just don't have a collective belief system or community that recognizes the calling for what it is. Thus, our calling is usually cloaked in spiritual emergency, which those around us see as emotional distress, and/or physical or mental illness. Because we view such through a lens of judgment, our spiritual awakenings are more private. We don't talk about them, and we certainly don't put them forward as catalysts in changing our worldview. For this reason, our initiatory crises are less likely to be accepted as a spiritual awakening amongst our peers. In many cases, we, ourselves, don't realize crisis as a calling. This lack of community awareness and support is part of the reason that modern shamans don't get the cred of surviving baptism by fire that traditional shamans do.

While our personal dramas may occur in front of our loved ones, our inner initiations often do not. We shield the people around us from our spiritual crisis to avoid being judged as psychologically unfit, or for having backslid from our religious upbringing. In tribal cultures, the initiatory wound is not only witnessed by the group, moving through that pain is a collective effort. Under the wise hands of an elder shaman, the tribe trusts the process to produce a capable mystic successor. This difference in social structure not only shapes the process by which one becomes a shaman through support and witnessing, it also allows the budding shaman to be recognized as such more readily than our contemporary isolation.

In any culture, the new shaman must prove commitment as well as ability. Modern shamans frequently don't have that benefit of community recognition of our calling, thus proving status with the spirit world through the demonstration of our work and its results is key.

That said, most modern seekers find shamanism of their own volition, usually through a personal challenge, such as:

- Intuitive experiences that fall outside the current belief system (visitations from spirits, prophetic dreaming, lucid dreaming, connection to animal or Nature Spirit)
- Personal interest
- Need to live closer to Nature
- Feeling called by an experience of awe/changed life view
- Resolving spiritual emergency/trauma

Regardless of how seekers come to shamanism, a vast majority taking all routes cite a classic pattern in their shamanic emergence:

- Calling/Initiation/Crisis
- Death
- Resolution to proceed
- Acquiring helping spirits /Bestowal of power
- Recognition by the community/Shamanic role established in the community

It's important to note that most of this process is internal, reliant on strong inner guidance of the individual, regardless of external support. However, in order to be effective as a shaman, one must be recognized as such. Community is required. Without that recognition, the process that came before is moot.

What do you think?

What emphasis do you place on community in your spiritual path? In what communities do you actively participate? How do they feed you? What do you give back to them?

Consider your personal power. How important is it to you that your personal power be recognized? How might your spiritual path broaden with recognition from and interaction with others?

PART II – THE RELATIONSHIPS

Everything in shamanism is about relationships—the relationship to self, Spirit Guides, totems, the trance state, spirit worlds, sacred space, tools for journey, the journey itself, and community, and the change evoked, both internally and externally. In this way, the shaman does nothing alone, yet is constantly the initiator, the leader, the one responsible for evoking the relationship. Within the bond between shaman and soul work shaped our most profound understanding of animism.

Learning the Ropes

Apart from personal healing, it's no secret that a big draw to shamanism for many is learning ecstatic journeying. Journeying, or willing an aspect of the soul to travel into the spirit realm, is liberating, healing, and sublime. The thing is, it can also be scary, unhinging, and daunting. Many modern shamanists come to the practice with tunnel vision, to learn only the mechanism of the practice, itself. Without the proper grounding and understanding what journeying is, without clear instinct in how to navigate the spirit world and return to waking, embarking on that travel can create spiritual emergency. The process of learning ecstatic trance without proper respect can actually exacerbate the distress that brings many to shamanism; thus, it creates new trauma.

For that reason, I advocate learning to journey in a mentorship with a practicing shaman. It isn't impossible to learn to journey in a weekend class or from a book. It's that such hyper-distilled settings can't convey how to process what comes out of it, or deal with how it reshapes everyday life. Maintaining an ongoing mentorship over a period of time, with a shaman who is skilled and available, is imperative to truly learn and internalize soul travel.

What follows is an introduction to the various components of relationship that come into play as the relationship to journeying forms. By assessing these various components and how to work with them before delving into soul travel, allies are brought to the practice that will improve the experience of it.

Rituals

There is no one way to induce the space needed for shamanic journey, nor is there any specific requirement in shamanic work to do so. However, to undertake shamanic ecstasy without creating sacred space is akin to a surgeon arriving at the operating room without equipment, technicians, or nurses. I don't prescribe a specific way to achieve ritual or ceremony, but offer the criteria of shaping both as personal process emerges in shamanic journey.

Crafting ritual and ceremony are highly personal acts, with limitless applications. The information I share on rituals and ceremonies can pertain to the creation of them for any occasion. My purpose in introducing them here is to focus on preparation for and assimilation of shamanic journey. The focus isn't to make the ritual the same every time, but to sense what is the right ritual for each individual occasion, a skill that takes practice and time.

"Sacred space" is another way of saying "with intention." It isn't that through a ritual an ordinary room suddenly becomes alive and engaged in the magickal experience because we asked it to. From my vantage point, the room was already alive and magickal before anyone entered it. All space is sacred, all the time. Because we acknowledge its presence and significance through ritual and purpose, the room and everything in it becomes part of the ritual, part of the work. By honoring the elements of space, they become participants in our work. With them engaged, our work becomes intentionally sacred.

That said, I feel the creation of space to prepare to journey is imperative. It creates a distinction between our mundane and sacred, prepares the brain to shift into trance, and allows us to engage the elements to assist us in travel. As the approach to journeying refines, the mind starts to anticipate the signals of each step making the transition into trance easier and assimilation of the info acquired deeper. Eventually ritual may not be needed to move into or out of trance, though there are other reasons that implementing ritual is important. Ritual relaxes us, helps us focus, and fortifies our ability to carry intention through to the completion of the journey. Likewise, though ceremony may not always be necessary, it encourages us to celebrate and accept sacred support. It reminds us we're not alone.

Distinction between ritual and ceremony is important. Some use the words 'ritual' and 'ceremony' interchangeably, though there is an elegant distinction. In his book, *Sacred Ceremony*, Steven Farmer sums it best: "Ritual is something that we do in order to call upon or beseech the forces of creation to act on our behalf. Ceremony is the inspired expression of our dance with creation."[9]

Generally speaking, rituals are formulated sequences of gestures intended to bring about a desired outcome. The use of a rattle to call in the directions, drumming to shift brain states, using copal to cleanse the etheric field, or walking barefoot in grass are examples of rituals. Ceremonies are more open, centered around honoring personal connection with the Divine, celebrating the alignment of personal divinity with Source. Nature Spirit dancing, shapeshifting, acknowledging spiritual help with a life achievement, or releasing the spirit of a deceased loved one are ceremonies. Understanding the intention for creating a link between worlds clarifies whether devising a ritual or a ceremony is appropriate. Likewise, depending on the intention of the journey, how we open the sacred space to do so is a determining factor for which approach is used.

Generally speaking, why bother? Why take the time to create structure around a skill that for some of us is already innate? The short answer is discipline. Another is the awareness of what's available to us all; instilling readily available to us all, and instilling a regular framework for journeying can awaken that knowledge. Ultimately, I think Brant Secunda says it best, "The role of the human being is to maintain the balance between Earth and sky... Our prayers help to nourish the spirits. Ceremonies empower the Earth."[10] We implement rituals and ceremonies because we have a deep yearning to, and because doing so replenishes us all. This is yet again one of those animistic places where give and take between humans and spirits is a requirement.

There are many reasons that observing ritual as a prelude to shamanic journey is significant. Foremost, shamans believe that the components used in creating space, opening a circle, or calling in the directions as it may be called, are alive themselves, and help to hold the space for work. We don't have to do it all, or alone. These helping spirits share the burden of creating the atmosphere for work and of doing the work, itself. Not only is carrying out the intent of the journey a communal effort, so is its preparation.

It has been readily observed, however, that the components of ritual serve therapeutic and psychosomatic purposes, as well. Certain stimuli, such as repetitive sound or flickering light affect brain waves, which allow us to move into and out of varying degrees of trance. These triggers also root us better into the trance experience, and permit better retention of the information we learn while there. Other components, such as specific scents, textures worn, trance postures, or fetishes (power items) trigger sensual responses that promote physical calmness or a quietness of mind. These creature comforts can help us better assimilate the wisdom gained from soul flight.

Perhaps the most practical reason for creating ritual leading into journey is to give ourselves permission to leave the waking world. I find that because we Westerners don't bring mindfulness practices into our daily lives, we don't know how to release into special sacred experiences. Ritual is our opportunity to leave behind concerns and insecurities, and allow the elements and spirits of the surrounding space to be escorts to Otherworldly destinations.

Begin setting the precedent to willfully, joyfully fly out by tuning the journeying area and the items in it to that purpose. The arrangement of items in the area as well as colors in it may be relevant. Clothing or ritual garb worn may be important. Physical expression of the space and spirits in it by dancing, singing, or toning may help. Such observation of and participation with etheric detail not only creates a subliminal intention to begin relaxing and departing the waking world each time ritual for journeying begins, it becomes part of the intention bolstering the whole process.

In that way, crafting ritual or ceremony is an area in which having a grounded footprint of textbook knowledge of certain fields, such as geology, herbs, animals, or trees can be very helpful. The subsequent section, *Tools,* discusses the many components of journeying and using them in ecstatic work more fully. The more knowledge one has of the manifest world, the more easily one connects with and attains its spiritual counterpart. It is not a requirement to study a mundane field, but it can be very practical. Even informational resources can be spiritual allies.

Neurologically, ritual and ceremony work by creating a shift in brain waves. Using a machine called an electroencephalograph to measure the frequency of brain waves, it is documented that certain scenarios and stimuli affect brain function.[11]

A Note on Brain Wave States

The primary focus for journeying is on the theta brain wave state. Deep cognizant trance occurs in the theta state. This is considered a "god" state, in that in this state we are connecting with All That Is on a deeper conscious level, without the distractions and insecurities we have in the waking state. Understanding theta is a bit easier in the context of daily activities and how the other states fit in.

Electrical activity in the brain is displayed in the form of brainwaves. There are four main categories of brainwaves, ranging from the most active to the least: beta, alpha, theta, and delta.

When the brain is actively engaged in mental activities, it generates beta waves. These beta waves are of low amplitude, and are the fastest of the four different brainwaves. The frequency of beta waves ranges from 13 to 30 cycles a second. Beta waves occur in our waking, engaged state, when we are conversing, teaching, working. Beta is awake, normal, alert consciousness.

The next brainwave division in order of frequency is alpha. Alpha brainwaves are slower, and higher in amplitude. Their frequency ranges from 8 to 12.9 cycles per second. Alpha is the state induced in hypnosis—it can be responsive, but isn't actively engaged. This is the state after having completed a task and sitting down to rest. It could also be meditation, the state induced in hypnotherapy. Alpha is a relaxed state, lucid, an absence of thought.

The next state, theta brainwaves, consists of greater amplitude and slower frequency. This frequency range is normally between 4 and 7.9 cycles a second, which occurs during daydreaming, deep relaxation, mental imagery, and deep meditation. Theta can be described as the state of driving, yet being unable to recall the last five miles.

The final brainwave state is delta. Here the brainwaves are of the greatest amplitude and slowest frequency. They typically center around a range of 0.5 to 3.9 cycles per second. They never go down to zero because that would indicate brain death. Deep dreamless sleep is the lowest frequency of delta, 2 to 3 cycles a second. At this level the unconscious mind engages.

A lesser researched state is gamma, which leaves it fairly controversial. That, of course, makes it worth mentioning here. Gamma is a brainwave state documented in extremely excited states. It ranges from 30 cycles and greater, and is the fastest brainwave state. Some are noted as having gone up to 100 cycles per second, though around 40 is typical. Bursts of insight and higher cognition are attributed to gamma, as are out of body experiences, psychic abilities, and seizures.

A routine scenario illustrating brain states would be: when we go to bed and read for a few minutes before attempting sleep, we are likely to be in low beta; we put the book down, turn off the lights and close our eyes during which our brainwaves will descend from beta, to alpha, to theta; and finally, we fall asleep and reach delta.

Theta, or cognizant dreaming, is the state entered into during shamanic journeying. A phrase often used in modern shamanic communities to describe this state is "nonordinary consciousness," shifting from waking consciousness to spiritual consciousness, from physical reality to metaphysical reality, from Earth to Spirit. Components of ritual, such as flickering candlelight and drumming, facilitate achieving theta brain state.

Why does brain state matter in terms of healing? In the theta state shamans observe that other levels of consciousness are more easily accessed and changed. For this reason, shamans often used drumming or other monotonous sound for soul travel. As well, they tend to work in dark areas inducing the sleeplike state of theta—tranquil enough to comfortably drift out, yet mindful enough to hold intention. In ritual, we slide between active brain states; we step between the worlds.

On a very practical level, engaging in ritual to shift consciousness activates both hemispheres of the brain. When we use both sides of the brain at once, we become both the Creator and the created. We become the force that shifts ourselves. Ritual draws on life force at a cellular level, to fully enmesh with the journey. In creating a ritual prelude to journey, every cell in the body comes to recognize the preparation for soul travel and will be ready for it. In ritual we are the active soul in form. While science supports the need for ritual, only personal exploration with it reveals the spiritual power of it.

Following are components for creating rituals:

Criteria

Ritual generally contains certain features, which serve specific functions. The following sections cover information on the criteria of ritual as a guideline for crafting personal process prior to journeying. The purpose of exploring these criteria is to determine how we relate to them, how we can incorporate them into creating sacred space, and thus how we work intentionally with All Things. Through these criteria we learn and create personal cosmology.

Cleansing

Clear the self and space by smudging with an herb or incense, or by spritzing gem elixirs, placing essential oils on the body. Affirmations can also be used for clearing.

Grounding

Using a rattle, breathing technique, visualization, guided meditation, or physical movement, prayer, etc., bring the self present. It is important to be fully present in the preparation for a journey. This allows the focus to remain on the intention for the journey, through its completion.

Creating Sacred Space

This is casting a circle, calling in the directions, or walking the medicine wheel through chanting, singing, dancing, visualizing a protective circle of light, or scattering a circle of salt or other significant element. There are infinite ways to do this. What's important is to experience the elements and directions to find the one that best speaks to us. This is a point that textbook knowledge could help focus otherwise limitless and overwhelming possibilities.

Calling in the Powers
Allow the spirits of the elements and directions to be present and supportive of magickal work. Calling in the directions doesn't mean the Powers weren't already there. It is merely grateful acknowledgement to the elements and directions for their ongoing support and guidance. In truth, it's calling our attention to the fact that the Powers are always there. Different cosmologies honor different elements and directions. For instance, in Eastern Cherokee cosmology, east is red, the element air, and relates to creativity. In Celtic spiritual traditions, circles were always opened from the east, following the sun's path. On the Cree Medicine Wheel, east is always yellow. Consider the following directions and elements:

East	Within
West	Fire
South	Water
North	Earth
Above	Ether
Below	Metal

Invoking the Deity or Deities
Some people feel an affinity to specific deities or kingdoms and call them in prior to journeying—the fey, Nature devas, archangels, saints, gods, goddesses, mythologies... Also, deities often correspond with a direction and/or element.

Tools

The most widely used tool in shamanic journeying is the frame drum, or hoop drum. It's handheld, can be made of any number of materials, and travels fairly well. As with all aspects of shamanism, relationship to the drum is imperative. For that reason, many shamanists make their own drums, evoking the drum's spirit and engaging with it during its creation.

It's not mere coincidence that drumming is associated with shamanic trance across time and culture. Tribal meetings around a flickering campfire combined with steady drumming trigger cellular memories in us all. Together, they create a hypnotic daze, luring us into the adventure of the theta brain state.

How the drum is used varies widely. We discussed earlier in the section on *Rituals* the importance of brain state and how various tools influence it. Most pervasive is drumming 3-4 beats per second to attain the theta state. However, technology has given us binaural drumming, in which two tones similar in frequency are played, one in each ear. The brain responds to the difference between the two, which creates a theta state. The Internet makes it possible to try these various drumming approaches in small samples. Do a quick search on "shamanic drumming," and "binaural drumming," then test them out. I suggest starting with a basic 3-4 beats per second tempo, and explore from there to determine which best facilitates theta.

For decades, I've used drumming, 3-4 beats per second, for journeying. I always opted for technical assistance by way of a recorded drumming track, as drumming while I journey is not my forté. The act of drumming serves as a distraction to my trance experience. A drum track on a CD or digital music player is a perfectly modern yet viable solution to not having a live-in drummer. Whether comfortable doing so via headphones or with the sound ambient throughout the room, take time to gauge the effect of various sounds on the ability to move into trance. Some people are adept at drumming for themselves as they journey. Give it a try, and if too many synapses are sparking to allow proper trance, go the route of a recorded drum or sound track.

In recent years I find the sound of a drum in my personal journeys distracting. So internalized is the cadence of the drum that I hear it upon intention, and so thorough is my opening of space, that when journeying for myself, I don't use the drum at all anymore. Evolving to different uses of sound is fine, as long as the preferred method assists trance.

Although rare, I've had clients who couldn't bear the drum from the start. Instead of lulling them deeper, it wound them up, taking them into an anxious beta state. Should drumming not soothe, or if you would like to explore other sound inductions to trance, possibilities are the rattle, didjeridu, toning, and chanting. Again, search for samples online and give them a try to see how they affect calmness.

While drumming has its place, rattling has a specific purpose in my process, as well. I find that the rattle brings me present like no other trick. It works every time. I can just rattle willy-nilly and feel my etheric field shifting to a calmer state, or I can employ specific rhythms to change the space around me. As well, rattling is part of my ritual to create space. In that way it meets both needs of shifting my life force, and engaging that of the space around me.

To tie up a few tips on drumming, consider the cues it must supply. If using a sound track for journeying, make sure it specifies a callback. Callback is a short break after the trance tempo, followed by a louder, extremely rapid tempo. In short, callback is obnoxious and annoying, as it means the party's over. That is its whole purpose. Callback signals that it's time to extract oneself back to waking, and it tells the brain to shift gears back to a calm alpha brain state. When drumming to induce trance, it's still good practice to acknowledge callback. Listen to a few examples online to get an idea of how to do it, and how to time the signal accordingly.

Staying in trance until the callback isn't mandatory. If the intention is fulfilled and the callback hasn't sounded, return from the journey anyway. Often when we stay past the point of necessity, we begin to lose focus on why we were there to start with. For that reason, always retreat from journey when the objective has been met, regardless of callback.

If callback sounds before the intention is fulfilled, it's fine to continue to journey further with the regular tempo. Just restart the device or continue drumming. However, if a great deal of time has lapsed and the objective hasn't been met, particularly if the journey doesn't seem to progress, retreat from trance. There is no timeframe for which soul work should be completed in journey; though remaining in trance without progress indicates a need to refine the process. Perhaps the intention isn't well-crafted, or more care in how to navigate is needed. When feeling stuck in a journey and restating the intention doesn't provide movement, return from trance, and consult a mentor on ideas for progressing in soul travels. Also, the subsequent section, *Journeying Tips* covers a few possibilities for why journeying doesn't progress.

Power items, Fetishes, and Altars

Don't we just love accessories? Certainly there are many reasons we're attracted to certain adornments, colors, fabrics, clothing styles, fragrances, logos, and bling. Comfort, sense of style, self-expression, and cultural identity are just a few of the reasons that we incorporate trinkets into how we present our person. In short, we accessorize because our lovelies enhance our sense of power in some way, and this is also true of shamanic power items.

Called fetishes, talismans, medicine bundles, or mesas, these items are tools that perform a tactile purpose, though they also serve as spiritual allies, conductors, and heavies that help us hold the space for journeying. These can be anything from animal parts to feathers, swatches of fabric with meaningful design and color, herbs, divinatory tools, candles, leaves, twigs, sigils, likenesses to deities, crystals, stones, religious artifacts, incense… It's also valid to incorporate items that aren't considered sacred in a broader sense, though on a personal level have deep meaning. If it holds power to us, it's a fetish in our shamanic work. The possibilities for power items are endless, and as unique as ourselves.

So we've got this woo woo collection. What do we do with it? Placing items on an altar, prayer mat, or shrine is a typical presentation. Arrange them in a way that supports connection with the elements of the space and the directions, how they best present when assembled together, and in a way that keeps them in the working area without creating an obstacle course for those who pass through it.

My fetishes are arranged on various cloths, all of which change seasonally, and depending on the purpose for the journey. Likewise, the components of my sacred center change, too. I generally keep a candle on my mat, stones from a significant place, and sprigs of Nature allies currently growing in my garden. Among my more unusual fetishes are a ticket from Tori Amos' first solo tour, a deer jawbone artfully enlivened by a friend, my precious carved owl, a bright blue scarf with the Newgrange triskele on it, and a card my mother gave me when I was six years old.

Include as fetishes what holds power. Understanding how that influence affects personal power and space is significant. For instance, some people want their power items to be visible and accessible during the journey. Others dedicate a corner or out-of-the-way area as the shrine of their home. For me, the placement of my altar is important. Mine goes in the center of my work space. I want it to be in the heart of the room, visible by all involved, unobstructed by clutter or vanity. There's no right or wrong in the creation of sacred space. Details that work for the shaman and the space express precisely how it should be.

Taking power accessories a bit deeper, some shamanists are required by their guides to make their ritual tools and acquire their fetishes naturally. Others are more of the mind of sacred shopping—putting out the intention that the power items most needed will make their way to us, and recognizing when they do. Again, what works best for each individual is the right way. If uncertain of how to acquire, evoke, and work with ritual tools and fetishes, open this conversation too with Spirit Guides in journey. Allies will manifest in no time!

What do you think?

Observe items that you keep near, whether in your work or personal space, as well as ones that you carry on your person. They may be a stuffed animal from childhood, a book your grandmother gave you, a picture of yourself as a child, or a souvenir rock from a camping trip. What makes them special to you? Are you comfortable with letting others touch or hold them?

Take some time to record the history of five items you keep near, noting how you acquired them, the roads they've traveled with you, and what significance they hold to this intense relationship.

After completing this mini-memoir, write a similar history from the perspective of those items. Note your importance to them, and allow their experience of you to come forward. What commonalities or differences impress you in their story? What needs might they have of you?

Totems

We've established that animism is the perspective that all things have a soul, and that shamans are intermediaries who communicate with spirits by leaving their bodies to travel into the spirit world for healing of self, another, or a community. Where shamanism is an expression and exploration of animism, totemism is perhaps Nature's best-shared tool for being an effective animist. Evidence of totemic relationships exist in many cultures, worldwide, and one truth that bonds them all is that your totem(s) chooses you, not the other way around.

The word 'totem' comes from the Ojibwe word 'odoodem,' meaning "his kinship group," though the observation is found throughout ancient and indigenous cultures. [12] Totemism is the observation of a spiritual or magickal connection between a human and an animal, plant, element, minerals, and perhaps other beings. Even life at the microbial level is regarded as totems for some. Other words heard in conjunction with totemism are: animal guides, medicine/power allies/animals, and familiars. Most often totems are animals, or Nature Spirits, though some approach them as spirit beings without specific characterization. My personal experience centers quite a lot on plant and elemental spirits, and in that light I encourage others to be open to their understanding of and work with totems. Why limit the help offered by spirits? Because I find totems can range in manifestation, I refrain from calling them "animals" and refer to them generally as "Nature Spirits." This is my preference and one that could conflict with the shamanic teachings of others.

It bears noting that totemism for some is valuable without the emphasis of shamanic work. That is, totemism can be studied without exploring the range of techniques shamans use. Nonetheless, in this text, I approach it in the context of working with totems in shamanic ecstatic soul travel, with the potential to develop lifelong relationships with them, and the ability to retrieve them for self when necessary.

What exactly are totems? The answers to this question range as much as the definition of shamanism. Some regard totems as an extension of the individual's psyche. Others consider them angels or spiritual manifestations of the natural world. They are perhaps best available to the human psyche as archetypes, with "their own qualities and characteristics [reflected] in the behaviors and activities of the animals."[13]

Having an animistic perspective, I regard Nature as the highest and most available expression of spirituality in the Earth realm. In that light, totems are conduits between the greater spirit realm and the human mind. For us they embody a certain safety through which we can experience the spirit realms, but also greet spiritual philosophies and concepts that we might otherwise not be open to or be able to process. By working through their characteristics, habits, and wisdom, we shed presuppositions and fears of spirituality and experience it in a more pure, open way. In short, we can deal with some truths better from a feathered, furred, or flowery friend than we could from a being more akin to our own physiology and presumed domestication.

An interesting observation in modern shamanism deals with that of insects. Contemporary shamanists often don't work with them, and outright refuse them in journey. I find this to be a personal matter, as certainly for every shamanist who refuses a totem, there's another who thrives in partnership with it. Some cultures don't work with spiders, while others will not engage with ravens. Digging into cultural connections to various totems sheds insight into why such reservations exist. How can we know what totems are right for us? Consider how a totem feels. As with all things in the realm of spirit, if it feels unsavory, it is, at least for the time being. Maybe at a later time, a discomfiting totem will be more approachable. This concern is a place in intuitive and etheric development at which having a mentor who has observed and attended our progression with totem relationships and journeying can give informed insight into whether a particular totem (or guide) is right.

Totems serve to educate humans on several levels. From a practical standpoint, they teach us about animal, plant, or elemental behavior, habitat, nutrition, social relationship, and even purpose. They teach us the ecology of specific regions, as well as the relationships between creatures of a region or regions, how they influence their habitat, thus influence each other and us. They teach us how our lifestyle impacts their ability to live healthily.

Mythology and lore often surround totems, making it difficult to cull fact from legend. In most cases, both serve to educate, as the symbolism of totems inform us on their historic, cultural or regional relevance, and how we have created archetypal relationships to those. Their grounded characteristics teach us survival across time. Through cultivating an understanding of a totem's history we come to understand its function in the present, as well as identify the points of intersection in our own biological development.

With more practical awareness of a totem, spiritual insights are perhaps more vivid. It is entirely possible to have a relationship with a totem and not study its formed existence. However, I highly encourage researching the mundane characteristics of totems. There may be mannerisms specific to a totem that are unidentifiable, but could influence the way we communicate with it. For instance, if a totem is a whale, it could be important to distinguish the slapping of its pectoral flippers as an expression of arousal, as opposed to a warning of aggression. Likewise, it could be useful to know that a Wild Turnip totem switches gender depending on where it is in its growth stage or that some reptiles' gender is selected by temperature. I know "homework" is the last thing anyone wants to hear, though sometimes small details that stump us in deciphering totem communication can be easily resolved with a bit of research.

Likewise, I caution about depending solely on outside sources as the basis for establishing a relationship with a totem. While learning the overall mannerisms of a species is beneficial, it is not a replacement for connecting with the specific totem visiting us, to learn expressly what it needs us to know. This observation includes working with totem dictionaries, as well. While the scientific, historic, and archetypal understandings of them enlighten in profound ways, the personal relationship with the specific totem visiting us is where the deeper connection begins and thrives.

In addition to transmitting knowledge, working with totems within a shamanic context permits them to assist in holding sacred space. Often in preparing for ecstatic journey to the spirit realms, shamans call upon their totems—or a particular totem when performing specific work—to aid in attaining the state of trance itself, to reach the desired destination, etc. The emphasis on the power of the totem in creating ritual reinforces its bond with the shaman, as well as facilitates how the shaman's work is done.

Many people feel that wearing the guise of their totems deepens their bond with them. For some this means donning full regalia in honor of that totem, while it can mean simply wearing furs, tails, ears, petals, fronds, leaves, scales, etc., and giving them a voice, letting them dance through our bodies. Eschewing the wearing of totemic items, some are more comfortable merely placing fetishes about their workspace, or on shrines to honor Nature Spirits.

In the case of animals, there can be conflict around the use of biological material for totemic purposes. Obviously personal choice is a factor, as is determining humane sources of such materials. Totemism doesn't require working with animal parts. In fact, if drawn to work with animal parts, plants, or feathers, be aware of regional legal constraints upon such. In lieu of biological material, a drawing of a totem or other replica can suffice. A recording of its song can inspire. There is no requirement to have a likeness of a totem(s) in ritual or personal space, though by honoring them in some physical way, the relationship with them is anchored into day-to-day interactions. It becomes part of the earthly consciousness.

Most people, along their work with totems, begin to feel a responsibility to give back to these Nature Spirits. For some it is a very literal act of caring for the local animals or plants—feeding one's own garden visitors or those of a public space. Others volunteer in shelters or reserves dedicated to compassionate wildlife or domestic intervention. Even just volunteering to clean litter from a park or reserve is a great way to support Nature. The symbolism of leaving decadent treats on an outdoor altar in an act of sacrifice can also have deep meaning. (It can also invite unwanted wildlife, so share thoughtfully.)

What is important, though often forgotten in modern totemism, is the reciprocity of the relationship. These Nature Spirits want to have a relationship with us as much as we need to bond with them. Ceremony—the celebration of the sharing relationship—is what creates beneficial outcomes for both.

Totems and Purpose

"Yeah, yeah yeah," I often hear. "That's all great and informative, but how do I meet my totem?" Well, there are many ways to find a totem, and most seekers likely have several to meet. A more refined question may be, "Which totem do I most need at this time?" Sure, we likely have a primary totem that stays with us for the duration, but many others come to help us with different needs.

Recall that totems choose us, which makes forming relation-ships with them critical to working with them. In forming relationships we acquire not only an ally for our own needs and growth, we also form a lasting bridge between the spirit world and the formed world. We become the correspondent to the Nature Spirit on events in formed reality, while the Nature Spirit shares insight on Nature and the spirit realm. Within this relationship anything is possible—education, divination, healing, time travel…

What distinguishes a random visit from a Nature Spirit versus the long-term partnership with a totem? I believe that is revealed through ongoing exploration of the Nature realm. The more we engage with it in a knowing fashion, using all senses and awareness available to us, we begin to discern how to connect dynamically with the space we're in (wherever we are, wherever we go), how to interact with the Nature Spirits there, and to forge relationships with those who seek to work with us. Remember that regardless of the role Nature Spirits play in our lives, the effort in forging those relationships enhances the wellbeing of All Things.

Also, as is true with Spirit Guides, some totems are with us only for a short time. Their purpose is to foster us through a life transition, after which they move on. Others come to focus attention on a specific study or need. For instance, practitioners who do energy work may call in a totem for each chakra, or to help with a specific concept, such as compassion. The totem aids in that finite arena, only.

Likewise, we can call in totems for very specific needs. For instance, each chakra has a totem. Progressing through working with each, call in its totem. Similarly, when determining personal cosmology and how to work with it, call in a totem to assist. Many shamanists call in a totem for each direction or fetish on their altar.

I've never met someone who didn't have Nature allies, usually several. I often encounter people who firmly believe their totem to be their favorite cat, or because they've always loved zebras, that must be their animal guide. Be open to the infinite possibilities in greeting Nature Spirits. Often they aren't what we anticipate, yet other times are precisely as expected. Hold flexibility not only in the perspective on what totems are, but how they can come to us, and what work can be done together. My experience is that when we begin to become closed off in how we perceive our connection to our totems, we create dissonance in our spiritual travels, thus distance from our connection in All Things. By engaging totems and connecting with Nature, we move closer to our own divinity.

What do you think?

Does a shaman have to be a totemist, or vice versa? How do these roles complement and/or contrast?

With what Nature Spirits do you feel a connection? Have you had close contact with these creatures? What was that like?

What elements of Nature appeal to you that you hadn't considered to be totems? Could they be?

What totems are prevalent in your culture (national bird/flower/crest)? How do they influence your spiritual work or Nature appreciation?

How do you honor totems in your spiritual work? In your daily life?

Consider ways that you can give back to the Nature Spirits who work with you. What gestures come to mind?

Spirit Guides

Meeting a Spirit Guide is probably the most defining moment on the shamanic path. I recall the first time I met mine, an older man akin to Merlin, a silver sage wrapped in a gossamer frock. My feelings were a mix of familiarity, surprise, and awe. I've heard guides called many things—"angels with archetypes," spirit teachers, guardian angels—though the role is clear across cultures and time: to shepherd the living.

As with Nature allies, some Spirit Guides are permanent. They are with us for the long haul of this life, and perhaps beyond, or before. Others, I refer to as spirit helpers, who are with us only for a short time, to lead us through a life transition. Often we encounter helping spirits when we change jobs, move house, end a relationship, or start a new routine. They midwife through change then retreat back into the ether. In rarer instances, some of us have more than one Spirit Guide, each managing specific tasks or supporting explicit needs.

A common concern among clients and students is not having a Spirit Guide. Often they have tried various means of communication to no avail, and are concerned that they're alone in their spiritual navigation. I've never worked with someone who didn't have a Spirit Guide. I have, however, worked with many people who resisted the guide who came. I've also fallen into the camp before, myself.

As with totems and Nature allies, we often think that because we are of a particular background or feel a connection to a specific culture or life experience, our guide will correlate with that fondness. Be open to the beings that respond to intentions to meet Spirit Guides. It may not be the culture or tradition expected, which may directly correlate to wisdom that guide has to share, or skills to teach. Often mythic figures or deities come as guides, and there is a tendency to feel ego pulls around such celebrity. Remember that our guides (and totems) shape to what can best reach us. Maybe an Incan Tiahuanaco god shares with a shamanist secret mystery information about Lake Titicaca. Maybe we are all receiving that universal information within relevant contexts. Maybe it's all metaphor about realizing hidden personal potential. That's the beauty of working with guides—their blessings can bring power in many forms. We see that best when we get out of their and our own way.

A question that often comes up is, "Is my Great Aunt Thea my Spirit Guide?" Perhaps. Determining guides is a very personal experience. I've known loved ones to provide personal guidance, though they tend to appear as helping spirits rather than long-term guides. Generally speaking, seeking loved ones out as guides is tricky. Traversing the spirit worlds is challenging enough to the psyche without bringing in emotional involvement. When we seek guidance from loved ones—deceased or living—in journey, we run the risk of blurring boundaries, thus, we compromise our ability to remain focused on our intention and fulfill the healing that is needed. I won't say it's not possible, though more often than not, working with loved ones as guides isn't practical regarding our overall needs.

Guides aren't here to do our work for us, or to be our personal oracles. Sure, they may fill both of those needs on occasion. Most likely, they will challenge us in how we do both of those things for ourselves. At best, they are facilitators in fostering us to figure things out for ourselves.

What do you think?

Make a wish list of strengths you want your Spirit Guide to bring you. Be as detailed as possible.

Likewise, imagine what gifts you might bring to your Spirit Guide. For what reason are those particular blessings important for you to share?

What boundaries might you have in working with a Spirit Guide?

Consider traditions or cultural groups that you wouldn't want as your Spirit Guide. For what reason might you exclude them? For what reason would you more readily accept other traditions?

Shamanic Cosmology

As with most facets of shamanic work, there are many ways to honor and explore cosmology. Defined as how the origins and evolution of the Universe present themselves to us, our relationship to cosmology is the most important component of navigating spirit journeys. It gives us a way to put our journeys into meaningful context. Cosmology is our map to the spirit worlds. Without a sense of cosmology, we wander nebulously. Lacking the ability to direct ourselves, I'd say it's virtually impossible to fulfill the intention for soul travel.

For as many shamanic cultures as have existed, there are that many and more observations of the birth of the Universe. To Australian Aboriginals, through the Dreamtime, or Dreaming, ancestor spirits created the land and Nature. The Cherokee creation story entails a water beetle traveling from the sky vault of Galunlati to water beneath, dredging up mud that grew to become the great floating island, Earth. Norse cosmology includes nine worlds connected by the Yggdrasill, or World Tree. In all stories of universal origin are the observations of strata above and below, giving us some semblance of moving between worlds.

While changing vantage points in a cosmology can be taken literally, certainly metaphorically, a modern dialogue for the classic ascension to an upper world or descent to a lower world is movement between levels of consciousness. The ability to willfully adjust from the beta to theta brain state is an apt allegory of soul travel.

A triple cosmology, comprised of the Upper, Lower, and Middle Worlds, is common across many shamanic cultures and though I experience it more widely, is how I express soul flight. Because I reference it in this way should not pose any limits on how personal cosmology shapes or functions. Feel free to translate my approach into the structure and vocabulary that works best. If no sense of cosmology is observed prior to exploring journeying, work with the triple-world model, and remain open for a personal relationship to universal origin to engage as is best.

Lower World

The Lower World is the deeper well of Earth's magick. Pristine Nature filled with animal beings and plant helpers, it also hosts creatures of mythological and legendary status, such as the fae and elemental devas, as well as those that are extinct or unknown. Traditionally, most people meet their totems in this space, and do most of their work with them here. The Lower World is the place of memory and physical concerns, and is often associated with instinct and primal awareness. Healing is often focused on physical and emotional needs, though it's not limited to them.

Plants, rocks, trees, insects, animals, birds, the elements, the directions, and all of earthen life emerge as guides and helpers here. A certain comfort comes from the unified spiritual support of the Nature realm. This stratum is usually introduced as pristine, the presentation of Nature that is most needed. It is important to recognize that the Lower World has no affiliation with the concept of Hell. Not a place of punishment for one's choices, the Lower World is a place of perfect nature and nurture of the Self.

In the Lower World we begin tapping into Earth's spirituality, as in Earth as a soul, herself. We reconnect with her position in the galactic family, and through that connection widen our awareness of the planet and her role in our Solar System.

How we access each world is unique. Each realm has what is called a portal through which we enter, travel, then exit. A natural fixture, such as a body of water, an ant hill, or tree roots, leads down to a damp, cool passage opening to the Lower World.

Many know they have moved into the lower realm when they pass through a water barrier, such as a misty spray, a stream, or falling rain. This sensation is not a requirement for passage into the Lower World, but helpful recognition that grounds the senses and affirms lucidity without undermining trance.

In comparison to other realms, navigating the Lower World may be easier. Benefits are natural landmarks, and the ability to look across and take in the terrain. Even in landscapes of which we're not native, the instinctual drive to follow where we feel led kicks in. As well, often in the Lower World are power areas— rock formations, intriguing foliage, a captivating view. Noting such attention-getters can direct us to sacred space waiting for us in the Lower World. This attention to detail becomes very important as we implement the logistic framework of journeying.

Worth noting is that traditional shamanic cultures have tribal cosmologies, with which they are very familiar before learning to journey. The landmarks and figures they look for, which indicate progress along their travel, is evident to them. In a symbolic and perhaps very literal sense, they don't have to learn the ley of their soulscapes as they are learning to slip in and out of the spirit world. Modern shamanism differs for most spiritwalkers, in that most of us are learning both at once. We don't share a unifying cosmology; thus, we don't have the same sign posts to guides or indicate that we're on the right track. Cultivating these keen senses of direction and progress are imperative to the success of journeying, most definitely of facilitating soul healing.

Middle World
The Middle World is loosely considered the spiritual expression of the Earth. I think of it as Earth's astral self, our planet's unseen, its soul. The Middle World is the destination most closely related to our waking reality, in which suffering spirits linger, Nature Spirits dwell, dreams occur, the strata of beings we know as

faeries, elves, and sylphs, etc. reside, and provides a good place for observation of the Divine in our mundane lives. Where the Lower and Upper Worlds are pristine personal spaces, the Middle World is shared space, between all souls engaging in the earthly realm. Certainly all space is shared with perception biased by personal and cultural influences. As we are most closely tied to the Middle World, this space is presented as it is, with the understanding that personal filters influence how we perceive it. For that reason we often see "your Upper/Lower" World, and "the Middle World." The wording isn't necessarily relevant, though the instinct to 'claim' the Middle World is important. Because of this distinction, quite a bit of latitude can be taken in understanding the range of this middle layer, and the work that can be done in it.

Because we exist in the Middle World as spirits in form, we are very emotionally involved with it, and the experiences we have there often challenge our belief systems. Many of us have been programmed to fit certain paranormal experiences into categories of "good" and "evil," "positive" and "negative." Thus, visits in the Middle World can trigger crisis when they don't mesh with our beliefs or personal truths.

The challenge of doing work here is greater for most soul travelers because it is hard to release expectations of what we think it should be compared to how we experience it in form, what we have been told it is, and what benefit we should receive by engaging it. For this reason Middle World journeying wasn't touched on in-depth early in the Western shamanic movement, despite that's where most of us have our first experiences with the unseen. Indigenous shamans focus a great deal of their work with plant and animal helping spirits in Middle World relationships. A wider range of cultural approaches are taught now, many of which do include Middle World techniques.

Being a lifelong intuitive, my most formative exchanges with souls began in the Middle World, and inspired my book, *Real*

Wyrd – A Modern Shaman's Roots in the Middle World. I always teach journey to this earthly spiritual layer, though I present it in a very realistic light: create sacred space, engage guiding spirits, be flexible, honor personal limits, and confer with a mentor. I don't feel that we can gloss over the spirituality most immediately evident to us, though I present this space as one to tread in carefully and with seasoned guidance.

Accessing the Middle World works differently than the Lower or Upper realms, in that there is no set portal. By imagining oneself in a familiar setting, a recurring dream, or even a book or film, a point of entry and exit is determined, from which exploration is done to intention's content.

Upper World

The Upper World is often experienced as celestial, a bright cloud-filled sky. For some it is a dark, void-like expanse, or a fantasy land. It's the place of Spirit Guides, saints, ascended masters and teachers. This realm is transpersonal space, containing angelic humanoids and deities. Here, life philosophies are explored and challenged. For me this realm tends to be the place that healing is done on diverse facets of the soul, where etheric healing sources, and where the examination of soul histories, such as the Akashic Record, occurs. The Upper World is where I commune with beings I call the Light Counsel, who do not manifest into form, though oversee the Multiverse. As with the other worlds, there are no rules or guidelines about what is found here, though it is usually pristine, serene, and supportive. Given that, the Upper World is not a place of heavenly reward after death, though it is available to any who seek it, at any point in life.

Though different from the Lower World, certain creature comforts are found in the higher spiritual stratum, as well. The division of wisdom to an echelon above the mundane awareness of humans provides us with the feeling that someone above and beyond our means is in charge. It taps us into the understanding that we are connected to a spiritual force beyond Earth magick, yet affirms through our mastery of Earth magick that we can venture safely into further realms. It isn't uncommon for one's cosmology to reshape after exploring the Upper World, expanding the understanding of the Universe and one's significance in it. The comfort of a greater intelligence at work becomes quite evident in the Upper World.

The portal to the Upper World is usually accessed by climbing something upward, such as a tree, stairs, or a ladder. I access it by entering my heart chakra and ascending a spiral staircase through my crown. Announcement of entry into the Upper World often comes in the form of passing through a misty cloud barrier. As with the Lower World, this sensation is not a requirement for passage into the Upper World, but a reminder that engaging the senses with imagination can deepen the trance experience.

Once arrived, traversing the Upper World is more challenging than the other realms. In the Lower World, even on unfamiliar terrain, it's still possible to imagine the solid ground beneath our feet, or being carried by water. In the Upper World there often is no such support. Gazing over a blanket of fluffy clouds or stars glittering in dark space doesn't offer much in the way of a map. In this space, if there is discomfort conceiving of self outside the five senses, beyond three-dimensional perception, traversing can be panic-inducing.

For new spiritwalkers, the Upper World neutralizes physical comfort zones and demands fierce mindfulness. For this reason, feeling the motion and sensation of climbing up, quite often coupled with counting steps (Level 1, Level 2, etc.), gives the earthly consciousness footing to find its way. As rock formations or lofty views indicate places of power in the Lower World, by ascending levels or steps, certain layers will stand out as significant in the Upper World. Trust the inner GPS. When the need to explore a layer calls, stop there and restate the intention. Explore the area until its meaning emerges.

General Notes on Cosmology

Ultimately, there are no fixed rules; there is no singular method-ology for how to access the spirit realms. I do advise working intimately with cosmology to personalize it, so that how it is accessed refines for journey work. Cosmology is our ladder to the beyond. Often, students who recognize intuitive gifts or spirit communication and then approach journeying as a means of refining their skill, abandon cosmology as a framework for navigation. They think that if they can innately step into other realms without prompting, there is no need to acknowledge a structure for doing so. Some express that learning a way to navigate themselves dulls the intuitive experience. Without exception, my students who abandon following a formula to get started with soul travel burn out very quickly. They identify that their intentions aren't being fulfilled, and that the experience becomes stressful.

I am and will always be an advocate that seekers do what's right for them. I also encourage students to learn the technique fully and practice it daily to learn if it complements the personal approach to the sacred, as well as to ground it into the daily experience. They key things that working with cosmology does in spirit travel—being acutely aware of moving between the worlds—are to provide a means of staying on task in otherwise overwhelming work and to provide us a way to root the metaphoric experience into tangible, meaningful insight. Part of observing the spirit realms through our cosmologies as we do deep, transformational work is to engage both hemispheres of the brain, through storytelling symbolism fused with the analytical extraction of meaning from those stories. Both aspects must be present. Without the ability to bring those two compo-nents together, the story has no meaning. The journey becomes escapist wandering in the mind.

Through exploring the cosmology, know that often shortcuts from one world to another emerge. With increased familiarity of soul travel and holding consistent intention, we become intuitively aware of the best place to address our needs. While the direction may indicate work in one world, upon arrival it's possible to be led to a different world, one more suited to the intention. In my experience, this most often happens in the Upper World, with the intention revealed and discussed there, though healing is performed in the Lower World.

Middle World Journey—Learning Personal Cosmology

As within, so without. A beneficial exercise in creating ritual is to learn how we relate to the Cosmos. Some cultures or spiritual paths have very strict observations of cosmology, or how they believe the Multiverse works and their place in it. If a connection to a cosmology is already in place, it's still a good practice to reacquaint with the elements and spirits of the ritual space, particularly in situations like relocation, when aspects of the home space or family structure have changed, or seasons have shifted.

In this exercise be very flexible in approaching the relationship to All. The practice of becoming familiar with how we relate to the Multiverse is invaluable. Some view their observation of the cosmos as experiencing existence between worlds. For me it is more finding my place in All, experiencing that connection while still feeling my individuality. It is about being in the worlds I need to accomplish the work I need to. When we conceive of how we fit into the Multiverse and how the elements and directions align to support us, we can use this information in creating sacred space to better do our work.

A practical exercise I've found in many earth-based studies is to observe deep responses to how we feel in each direction of our familiar. Find a center point in the garden or favorite spot in Nature. This exercise can also be done indoors, if that is more comfortable. I believe the Nature connection is imperative, however, so do perch outdoors, if possible. Regardless of location, it's important to be in a place from which quiet observation of the surroundings can be made, and to have an understanding of the directions in relation to this space. (Or keep it interesting by going through the exercise without knowing the directions, note observations, then verify the directions after.)

Begin by facing North, and allow any observations of the North to come. How does facing North feel? What thoughts and emotions arise? What memories or body sensations pique? What sounds and colors flow through? Does a particular elemental affinity present with the North? What plants grow there? What animals pass through? Where is the sun/moon?

Note what strikes interest at every level about the North, and when ready, progress to the East. Take copious notes. If moved, draw the elements of each direction as they are experienced.

Make the same observations about the East, then progress through the South and West. If it feels appropriate, also consider the directions of Above and Below, as well as Within, and note the significances of each. If another element of direction presents itself, explore how it relates to this work.

After moving through each direction, observe the originating point of the circle. Which direction feels like the starting point? In the ritual of calling in the directions or casting a circle, it is often important to note the direction from which it feels most appropriate to start—moving clockwise through the directions, or counter clockwise.

What do you think?

What stories of creation move you? What facets of those stories draw you to them? If you have a spiritual or religious cosmology, do those creation stories complement or conflict with it?

Take some time to consider your personal creation story. How does Source reveal itself to you? How do you implement Source through your sacred work? Your daily experience?

Consider how your creation story relates to your experience of cosmology. Write a summary of learning your cosmology. Detail the cosmology, including elements of it that surprised you, and those that were familiar. Did you observe other elements or directions?

How did it feel to sit at the center of All Things? How does it feel to be the Cosmos?

Forming Intention

Ecstatic, or shamanic journey is the willed travel of an aspect of the soul to a specific destination with an intention held in mind. It is this emphasis on purpose and coming back to it throughout the intuitive process that distinguishes shamanism from other esoteric practices. The intention may be to meet an animal or Spirit Guide, work with a specific deity, receive healing or information, or to learn more about one's spiritual landscape. Apart from understanding personal cosmology for impeccable navigation through our soul story, having a clear intention is the key to understanding what it means in practical terms.

A few points to keep in mind when forming an intention are:

- *Simple is best.* Keep the intention to a short sentence.
- *Resist the temptation to form the intention as a question.* Statements are more affirmative, and direct.
- *Work with one intention at a time.* Journeying again to cover other subjects, or to take information from a previous intention deeper, is always an option.
- *Intend to remember the journey.* Quite often we are so taken aback by how the experience unfolds that we forget to remember what's happening. As well, our brain chemistry changes in trance, and it can become challenging to remember the wording of the intention.
- *Intend to allow the journey to unfold.* As with remembering it, bring the focus back by restating the intention, as a way to remain out of the way of the process. Many budding spirit-walkers find it useful to restate their intention when they feel stuck, or when their mind wanders.

It's okay if it takes a while to form an intention, and to create the habit of continuously relating the journey back to it. The ability to return to the intention repeatedly in trance is key to fulfilling its objective, tying each visitor and event in the trance back to the intention. All of these pointers seem to stack up to a fairly hefty intention, counterintuitive to the suggestion to keep them simple. Practice this framework in how to journey to internalize subtle elements of it. When that deep relationship blossoms, the freedom to take the adventure deeper, try it different ways, and incorporate original techniques comes naturally.

Depending on the intention, a destination for the journey is chosen—the Upper, Middle, or Lower World. Each world has compelling qualities of healing and wisdom. These qualities, thus the destinations, become entwined the more experience we gain journeying.

An intention for journeying can be anything. Beginning ones are often (in this order):

- I intend to meet my Lower/Upper/Middle World.
- I intend to meet my animal guide in the Lower World.
- I intend to meet my Spirit Guide in the Upper World.
- I intend to meet a familiar place (the tree in my front yard, Niagara Falls, etc.) in the Middle World.

Summarizing Intention

Not to put too fine a point on it, carefully consider the intention. Often the progression of the trance fails because enough consideration of the intention wasn't given. It should be detailed enough to encompass the need, yet simple enough to be easily remembered and restated. It may help to write down the intention before beginning, and keep it nearby for quick reference when journeying.

Clarifying the need and how to retrieve information about it in a way that gives meaning is critical. For that reason, resist asking questions, and craft statements. Often, questions limit the response we receive. Recall that guides are not here to do our work for us. They respond to exactly what we present, and usually nothing more, often cloaked in metaphor and symbolism. The personal details of guide relationships depend on each guide and the relationship, though I generally advise students to approach their guides as they would a four-year-old. For instance, asking a preschooler, "Why?" gets responses such as, "Because." "I don't know." "It rained." I recall once when I was in crisis, I was extremely upset to find my always-sunny Lower World cloaked in darkness. "Why is it dark?" I asked my guide, hoping his insight would soothe me. In a way, his reply did. He said, "It has to be night sometimes," as in, 'This is the way it is. Get yourself in hand, and let's walk through it together.'

The best response is when they give no response at all, and instead stare back in frozen silence, or they do something utterly unexpected. The first time I met my primary owl totem, I was working out my introduction when he launched himself straight at me, feet first, and decked me squarely between the eyes. I didn't know what to think of that, though when I opened my eyes, I was flying above my Lower World. I'd never experienced anything so empowering or fantastic!

Have an idea of exactly what information will move the healing process forward, and create the best way to present that intention. It isn't so much about asking the right question to get the wanted answer as it is asking the question that will elicit the most meaningful information. Consider the integrity wanted in answers, and ask questions of the same depth.

Only journey when the exact wording of the intention is set. Ambiguity in wording or understanding the intention will bring vague results.

When comfortable with the mechanism of journeying and the results of beginning intentions, more advanced ones may be:

• I intend to meet [insert Nature Spirit] in my Lower World, to retrieve a ritual for creating space.

- I intend to meet a helping spirit in my Lower World who can help me with _____.
- I intend to engage the fae in the Middle World for insight in healing ____.

Having mastered sliding to spirit worlds, it may occasionally be appropriate to have an open-ended intention. For instance, healing or insight may be needed, yet forming an intention around the need may be unclear. In such cases it's fine to set a more open intention such as, "I intend to visit [totem] in my Lower World to retrieve healing for this feeling," or "I intend to visit my Spirit Guide in the Upper World to gain insight into this relationship."

blot out light further.

- Comfort. Choose a space in which sit or lie comfortably, without falling asleep.
- Isolation. Choose a space free of disturbances, located so as not to cause disturbance to others.
- Boundaries. Consider whether this space must be dedicated solely to shamanic work. Some people find that shared space is disruptive, and require that no one enter their journeying area, even when it isn't being used.
- Time of Day. Choose a time of day that supports being rested and aware. Avoid journeying at times of the day that are most tiring, as falling asleep during journey can create distress. Likewise, journeying while highly excited can be unnecessarily challenging.
- Safety. Choose a space that is safe. Some people prefer to journey outdoors, in public parks, the wilderness, etc. Know the surroundings. Ultimately, journeying is a trance state, in which the normal functioning mode of consciousness is changed; thus, the ability to defend self may be compromised. Be aware of animals, humans, plants, weather, etc., that affect the safety of journey.

In the beginning, how often should journeying be done? At least once a day, though no more than twice a day to start. It's possible to journey more, though more important is taking the time to assimilate the wisdom gained from journeying, before venturing off into another area. I've known many adept spiritwalkers who would slip in and out of journey, zipping all over the place in the spirit realm, though they disregarded their mundane life. They didn't root the seeds brought back into formed, solid ways of being spiritual throughout their lives, not just while in trance. Approaching journeying in this way makes it an escapist pursuit, rather than a spiritual practice. Without integrating the insight from journeying and allowing it to ground into a changed life perspective, the process is incomplete and often instigates crisis. Take time to work with what comes in waking life *after* journeying, so that a balance of journeying, implementing, assimilating, then journeying again is maintained. With proficiency engaging in ecstatic trance, it's possible to encapsulate the process very efficiently; thus, it becomes possible to journey more often.

Another consideration in the logistics of journeying is related to inner space, which is an honest response to the question, "Does it feel right to do at this time?" Only journey when it feels appropriate, by which I mean be honest about your emotional, mental, or psychological state. Feeling compromised on these levels brings more problems than solutions when engaging trance states. If sleep-deprived or ill, ask someone else for healing ecstatic work. If under a doctor's or therapist's care, don't undertake journeying without discussing it with him or her first, and by all means, mentors should be made aware of mental or psychological conditions.

I also encourage students to begin refining their vocabulary based on how they experience the subtler nuances of journeying. For instance, the phrases "ordinary reality" and "nonordinary reality," as in everyday physicality and interaction is ordinary, while engaging spirits is not. That logic, thus language, has never made sense to me. None of it is ordinary. The most mundane experience of buying a magazine from a street vendor isn't ordinary. The vendor, the magazine, the aromas of the city, the Nature Spirits in the vicinity, my own heart are all complicit in creating that experience, and I'm aware of that. I always have been.

Likewise "the spirit world" doesn't quite do it justice for me, either. Therein lies an assumption that a boundary separates what is soulful and what isn't. Everything is spiritual. Even this book has its own life force. All perceptions of being are hallowed and sacred, capable of being intelligently engaged at any point, any moment. Find the most genuine way to express them in dialogue. The more effectively we talk about them, the more we give them power in our mundane. How we think about these concepts affects how they present themselves to us. The more accurately our language matches our perception, the stronger our connection to journey experiences becomes.

For me, it's pretty basic. What others call "ordinary reality" I refer to as "waking." It's simple and sweet, and for me carries no emotional charge. It implies a perception of reality that may still carry intense spiritual experiences, though I wasn't dreaming or in trance when they occurred. Likewise, I don't experience the "spirit world," just "the world."

That said, the older I get and the more I expand and express my spiritual path, "waking" doesn't quite cover it, either. Ah, words. Yet what powerful allies they are.

Using Our Tools

Having explored the various tools available, there is some familiarity with those that facilitate bridging into trance, and those that lead us out. With them in place, a typical beginning journey is to meet the Lower World. It seems a bit strange to emphasize meeting a landscape, though the frontiers that greet us in the spirit worlds are very important, very much alive. Forming a relationship to them is as important as those we create with our totems and guides. Our Lower World landscape can inform a great deal about our unconscious, our current state of mind or life concerns, as well as from what terrains we best draw strength, or areas in life that could do with some work.

If possible, have a drummer be responsible for pacing and timing the journey, or drum for self. Some have great success with it, while others listen to a drumming track. To reiterate the details on drumming:

Twelve to fifteen minutes is a good starting interval—long enough to allow fulfillment of the intention, yet not so labored as to languish in infinity.

When it's time for callback—the pause, followed by rapid, loud drumming—thank guides or totems, then re-trace the steps back to and through the portal. Backtracking is very important, not just to stay grounded in the framework of journeying, but to remember the events that took place. Backtracking helps to integrate the ecstatic experience into whole wisdom.

Take plenty of time returning. Often when we rush back, we lose the details that led us there to start with.

Passage back through the portal and opening the eyes indicates completion of the journey.

Sit with the experience for a few minutes.

Pre-Journeying Checklist
Let's revisit a good way to approach journeying, and verify that the following are in place:

- Set the intention.
- Open sacred space/opening ritual.
- Journey to the intended world.
- Complete the objective of the intention.
- Express gratitude.
- Backtrack from the spirit world.
- When completely back in the body, open the eyes.
- Close sacred space/closing ritual.
- Take notes.

Then What?
Thorough note-taking in the beginning can help connect us more with our personal mythos. Writing, drawing, painting, sculpting journey experiences deepens our relationship to the lively components of journey, and helps us manifest their life force in waking. The more we can bring that ethereal experience into form, the more support we will have throughout our waking to

recall the spiritual in all things. Specifically, we will feel the support of our guides and totems as we create them in form and distribute that art throughout our lives.

I'm a fan of making a few notes, but express the experience through other modalities of art as much as possible. Often when we journal about our soul travels, we become so obsessed with the details that emphasis on integrating the wisdom from them is lost. Along the lines of allowing journeying to become escapist, when we delve too deeply in what everything means, why it happened, what its name is, the purpose of rotating sunwise instead of widdershins, the exercise becomes externalized and mental, rather than internalized and spiritual. In short, it becomes egocentric. The deeper metaphorical meaning is lost.

Find the delicate balance in expressing journey experiences for personal record and interconnection. Noting patterns, recurrences, and shifts over time can inform of new intentions to present to our guides. With regular journeying, the degree of detail needed will become evident.

The Journeys

Following are very basic introductions to ecstatic journeys. Read through them, and with the characteristics of each spirit realm in mind, become familiar with the basic steps of the framework before going into trance. Each of these exercises assumes the opening of sacred space for each journey, that working with fetishes and space to support the journey has been accomplished, and that the space will be closed when journey work is complete.

Lower World Journey – Meeting the Landscape
Our first journey to the Lower World carries the intention simply to meet it: "I intend to meet my Lower World." Write it on a slip of paper and keep it nearby, should a reminder be necessary during the journey.

If you are drumming for yourself or someone is drumming for you, give this journey 12 minutes before callback. If you are using an audio track, choose one 12-15 minutes long.

Restate the intention aloud several times, until its wording sits comfortably with you.

Begin drumming/start the drum track.

Imagine the portal, and move downward through its tunnel, observing with all senses. Notice colors, textures, smells, temperature, the energy of this betwixt space. Moving down, feel how the environment changes.

Follow the tunnel until passage through a water barrier comes. Emerge into the Lower World, holding in mind the intention to meet it.

Note your very first observation of the Lower World. What feelings stir?

Observe the Lower World from the neutral space of the tunnel, or step out and explore.

Does a particular direction or landmark resonate with you? Is it day or night? Is the Lower World familiar, or an utterly foreign place? How's the weather? Take in as much detail about the Lower World as possible.

If progression becomes stagnant or you feel off-track, bring your focus back to the intention. Quietly repeat it several times until it restores focus.

Having comfortably engaged the Lower World, or when callback begins, thank this scape for its welcome, and begin re-tracing steps to the portal. Slowly move up through the tunnel, then emerge. Open your eyes, and return to waking.

What do you think?

Congratulations! You are officially a skywalker!

Describe your first impressions of this initial landscape of your shamanic narrative.

In what condition did you find its terrain? What feelings did visiting it stir?

How did you navigate the Lower World?

What might you do differently to finesse working in your Lower World in later journeys?

Lower World Journey – Meeting a Nature Spirit

Our next journey to the Lower World carries the intention to meet a main totem, or Nature Spirit, however this being identifies: "I intend to meet my primary totem in my Lower World." Write it on a slip of paper to keep nearby, should a reminder be necessary during the journey.

Prior to doing this journey, consider what information is needed from or about the Nature Spirit. Possibilities are what strengths it brings, its reason for choosing us to work with, how to incorporate its skills and abilities into our lives... Take these possibilities into journey one at a time, addressing them as is appropriate. Remember, keep it simple. Tangential details learned can become their own intentions to address later.

If you are drumming for yourself or someone is drumming for you, give this journey 12 minutes before callback. If you are using an audio track, choose one 12-15 minutes long.

Restate the intention aloud several times, until its wording sits comfortably.

Begin drumming/start your drum track.

Imagine the portal, and move downward through its tunnel, observing with all senses. Notice colors, textures, smells, temperature, the energy of this between space. Moving down, feel how the environment changes. Is it the same as before?

Follow the tunnel to emerge in the Lower World, holding in mind the intention to meet the primary Nature Spirit.

Note the very first observation of a Nature Spirit. What feelings engage?

Observe this being from the neutral space of the tunnel, or step out and explore.

Move through the Lower World as feels best to greet this Nature Spirit. Ask the Nature being if it is your primary guide. If it's a helper, allow its insight into what life transition it supports. If it's the main guide, open the dialogue that feels most appropriate.

If stagnancy occurs in the journey or it feels off-track, bring the focus back to the intention. Quietly repeat it several times until focus is regained.

After comfortably meeting and talking with the Nature Spirit, or when callback begins, thank this being for the wonderful welcome, and begin re-tracing your steps to the portal. Proceed slowly up, through the tunnel, then emerge. Open your eyes, and return to waking.

What do you think?

What are your first impressions of the Nature Spirit that visited you?

What feelings did visiting with it stir?

How was navigating the Lower World different the second time?

What work might you imagine doing with this spirit? Begin developing your grocery list of work that you can do in the Lower World, possibly meeting various Nature Spirits to help you with that work. Likewise, begin refining what role you play in manifesting the life force of these beings in waking.

What senses were most dominant in the Lower World experiences?

As always, be patient, and take your time, grounding the wisdom of each journey as you unpack them.

Middle World Journey – Meeting Nature

This exploration has two distinct parts: a Nature walk, followed by spirit travel. Please do them in the prescribed order.

Part 1 – In this waking observation, hold the intention of being aware of the immediate world at the height of the five primary senses: "I intend to observe all that I can through my five primary senses in the immediate space around me."

In a familiar Nature setting, such as your garden or a fond public park, choose a safe place as the starting point. Remember the starting point.

From that start point, take a walk of about 15 minutes.

Using only the five senses, take in the details of that walk. If something piques your attention, pause and notice its sensual qualities.

Continue along in this way, eventually rounding back to the starting point within the set timeframe.

Part 2 – Shortly after this tactile excursion, continue the second part of this adventure in a quiet, dark space. Hold the intention to revisit the previous Nature walk from the perspective of the Middle World: "I intend to observe my Nature walk from within the Middle World." Write it on a slip of paper beside to keep nearby, should a reminder be necessary during the journey.

If you are drumming for yourself or someone is drumming for you, give this journey 12 minutes before callback. If you are using an audio track, choose one 12-15 minutes long.

Restate the intention aloud several times, until its wording sits comfortably with you.

Begin drumming/start the drum track.

Imagine standing at the designated starting point of the previous Nature walk.

Take the walk again, this time with all senses attuned.

As poignant details are recalled, notice layers of them beyond the five sense experience.

Continue in this way, observing at all levels available, the land, animals, sounds, smells, plants, and any interesting interactions had along the way.

As with the Nature walk, at callback return to the starting point.

When ready, open your eyes. Take a few minutes to anchor back into your body.

Thank Nature for the experience.

What do you think?

How did the Nature walk differ from the Middle World observation? How were they similar?

What elements of both walks surprised you?

What aspects of the Middle World walk seemed already familiar?

How did it feel to experience the unseen of a place you know well in waking?

What senses were most dominant in the Middle World experiences? Consider how different senses employ based on the intention and location of the journey, and why that might be.

Middle World Journey – Shapeshifting

A prevalent exercise in connecting with Nature Spirits is animal or plant dancing, also commonly referred to as shapeshifting. When we shapeshift, we allow the Nature Spirit to use our physical faculties for expression. This may be to convey a specific message or insight; for our own educational purposes; to experience the form, life, and perspective of another species; or to give a spiritual being the opportunity to experience form. As such, allowing a spirit into the form is a wanted, controlled exchange. Shapeshifting is a beautiful way to engage Nature Spirits, as neurological processes are enlivened beyond what we can describe. In the exchange of shapeshifting, words truly fail. Through sharing our form we experience senses beyond our normal perception.

I caution students to step away from Nature Spirits who approach them in a defensive or antagonistic manner. If they feel predatory, are showing their teeth, growling, or otherwise displaying aggression, I don't advise working with such spirits at this time. This doesn't mean these beings are off-limits permanently. Rather, they aren't supportive beings to work with at this time.

Progressing to the next journey, carry your instincts, as well as intuition. Be ready to wield and surrender both, as you are led.

For this journey, choose a safe, familiar Nature setting, such as your garden or a fond public park. Find a secluded yet comfortable spot from which to take this flight. Allow the senses to quiet. Close your eyes and experience the immediate area through all senses.

This journey to the Middle World carries the intention to shapeshift with a Nature Spirit: "I allow the Nature Spirit in my immediate space that most needs to connect with me to step into my body." Write it on a slip of paper to keep nearby, should a reminder be needed during the journey.

If you are drumming for yourself or someone is drumming for you, give this journey 15-20 minutes before callback. If you are using an audio track, choose one 15 minutes long.

Restate the intention aloud several times, until its wording sits comfortably.

Breathe normally for a few breaths.

With awareness on your breath, take 4-5 deeper breaths, inhaling more slowly than usual, exhaling more slowly.

Request to hear the body's affirmation of being fully in it: "I allow and engage my body to affirm to me that my awareness is soundly in my form." Go with the wording that best addresses this need. As well, go with the first sensation, flicker, feeling, etc. that comes. This sensation is the signal from your body that all is well.

Begin drumming/start the drum track.

As led, allow the Nature Spirit that comes to retain full expression through your form. Let it move arms and legs, speak through the voice, interact with the surrounding space.

As needed, return to the focus of sharing form.

Should any discomfort arise in the exchange, ask the spirit to step out of the form.

Stay with this expression until callback, though you can return earlier if the animal leaves.

At callback, state to the spirit that you allow it to step out of your form.

Feel the separation moment.

Return your awareness to your breathing, taking 4-5 deeper breaths than you normally would, welcoming them and letting them pass more slowly than usual.

As you become more aware of your form, allow your body to present its signal that you are in it and all is well.

After receiving the signal, open your eyes.

Middle World Journey – Engaging Nature Spirits

For this journey, choose a safe, familiar Nature setting, such as your garden or a fond public park. Find a secluded yet comfortable spot from which to take this flight. Settle on a concern, philosophy, affirmation, or general insight on which a Nature Spirit can inform you. Allow your senses to quiet. Close your eyes and experience the immediate area through all senses.

This journey to the Middle World carries the intention to gain insight from a Nature Spirit: "I allow the Nature Spirit in my immediate space that can best inform me on _____ to come." Write it on a slip of paper beside you, should you need a reminder during the journey.

If you are drumming for yourself or someone is drumming for you, give this journey 15 minutes before callback. If you are using an audio track, choose one 12-15 minutes long.

Restate the intention to yourself aloud several times, until its wording sits comfortably with you.

Breathe normally for a few breaths.

Begin drumming/start the drum track.

Go with the first awareness of a Nature Spirit that comes to you.

Allow it to check you out, as feels comfortable. Likewise, if there are curiosities you have about the spirit, address them. Be open to the many ways it may communicate with you, and you with it.

When you feel a rapport with the spirit, restate your intention.

Stay with this interaction as long as feels useful. Allow the dialogue—literal or figurative—to flow as it will.

If it feels appropriate, enquire if this spirit is a helping spirit or guide to you. Ask what strengths or gifts it brings you. Ask how you can honor it as thanks for this exchange.

Allow mutual benefit from the interaction by asking, "What do you need me to know most at this time?"

At the completion of the interaction, thank the spirit and turn your awareness back to your body.

Focus on your breathing, taking 4-5 deeper breaths than you normally would, welcoming them and letting them pass more slowly than usual.

As you become more aware of your form, open your eyes.

What do you think?

What is the significance of the spirit who visited you?

Had you worked with this Nature Spirit before?

How did its insight and/or interaction assist you?

. Write your experience of this healing narrative from the perspective of the Nature Spirit. How does processing this experience in this way inform you differently on the insight that was given?

As you work with various Nature Spirits in your familiar and more ranging spaces, note those who seem to be informants passing through, and those who reach back to you. What distinguishes each?

What plans do you have for how to fortify these relationships?

Upper World Journey – Meeting the Landscape

Our first journey to the Upper World carries the intention simply to meet it: "I intend to meet my Upper World." Write it on a slip of paper to keep nearby, should you need a reminder during the journey.

If you are drumming for yourself or someone is drumming for you, give this journey 12 minutes before callback. If you are using an audio track, choose one 12-15 minutes long.

Restate the intention to yourself aloud several times, until its wording sits comfortably with you.

Begin drumming/start the drum track.

Imagine your portal, and move upward through it, observing with all senses. Count your steps up if it helps you to gain a sense of place. Notice colors, textures, smells, temperature, the energy of this between space. As you move up, feel how the environment changes.

Move upward until you pass through a cool mist firmament and emerge in your Upper World, holding in mind your intention to meet it.

Note your very first observation of your Upper World. How does it affect your feelings?

You may observe your Upper World from the neutral space where you entered, or you may venture out and explore.

Do you feel led in a particular direction? What features stand out? Is it light, dark, or some other shade? Is your Upper World familiar, or an utterly foreign place? Take in as much detail about your Upper World as you can.

If you feel stagnant in the journey or as if you've gotten off-track, bring your focus back to your intention. Repeat it several times to yourself until you regain focus.

When you have comfortably engaged your Upper World, or

when callback begins, thank this scape for coming to you and begin re-tracing your steps to your portal. Take your time moving down through your portal, then emerge, open your eyes, and return to waking.

What do you think?

What are your first impressions of the Upper World?

In what state did you find its terrain? What feelings did visiting it stir?

How did you navigate it?

How did your Upper World adventure compare to trekking to the Lower World?

Describe the senses that engaged for this journey. Were they the same as other spaces, or unique to this world?

What might you do differently to finesse working in your Upper World in later journeys?

What do you think?

What are your first impressions of the Spirit Guide that visited you?

What feelings did visiting with it stir?

How was navigating the Upper World different the second time?

Describe key characteristics of your guide. What of those details surprised you?

What work might you imagine doing with this spirit? How might the life force of the Upper World assist with that work?

As always, be patient, and take your time, grounding the wisdom of each journey as you unpack them.

Upper World Journey – Engaging Your Spirit Guide

Our next journey to the Upper World carries the intention simply to allow healing from your Spirit Guide: "I allow my primary guide to heal _____." Write it on a slip of paper beside you, should you need a reminder during the journey.

Prior to doing this journey, consider what healing you wish to focus on. With beginning healing journeys, be open to new definitions of healing. It can be easy to bring in how we think healing should feel, look, behave, etc., and in doing so miss an opportunity to expand our understanding of it. When we limit our understanding of healing and how it manifests, we miss out on the healing, itself.

A good approach for healing journeys is to hold in mind feelings about what needs to be healed. When we think of what needs healing, our habit is to focus on a body area or specific physical thing that needs attention. Approaching it this way we remain focused on pain and assumptions about what alleviating it should be. Thus we limit what healing may be available. By directing the focus to feelings about what needs healing, we widen how we allow ourselves to receive healing. Approaching healing journeys in this detached yet personal way helps us alleviate expectation and remain focused on the fact that we are seeking to bring balance back to our life force, our lives. Healing isn't just about the alleviation of pain, or wanting to bring about a specific outcome. Balanced life force is the key to healing, and as we become more adept at how to allow and sustain that balance, symptoms on all levels of being eliminate.

Consider your feelings about something that needs healing in your life. This could be physical, emotional, mental, interpersonal. It could be a dynamic in which you are involved. Jot down three feelings related to that need, and form your intention for the journey. Remember, keep it simple. You can always go back later.

If you are drumming for yourself or someone is drumming for you, give this journey 15 minutes before callback. If you are using an audio track, choose one 12-15 minutes long.

Restate the intention to yourself aloud several times, until its wording sits comfortably with you.

Begin drumming/start the drum track.

Imagine your portal, and move upward through it, observing with all senses. Count your steps up if it helps you to gain a sense of place. Is it the same as before?

Move upward until you pass through a cool mist firmament and emerge in your Upper World, holding in mind your intention for healing.

Ask your Spirit Guide to come, then present your intention.

Engage your Guide as is appropriate to allow healing.

If you feel stagnant in the journey or as if you've gotten off-track, bring your focus back to your intention. Repeat it several times to yourself until you regain focus.

When you have comfortably met and worked with your Spirit Guide, or when callback begins, thank this being for coming to you and begin re-tracing your steps to your portal. Take your time moving down through the portal, then emerge, open your eyes, and return to waking.

What do you think?

How do you feel after this journey?

What did you learn about the healing need? Was the healing given what you thought it would be? Describe your first healing journey to the Upper World. Did you stay in the Upper World, or were other worlds involved in this healing?

What feelings did this healing stir?

Did this healing journey address the concern you brought to it?

How did the Upper World support this healing experience?

Consider ways to follow up on this healing, and what you can do to honor, thus, sustain it, in waking.

Journeying Tips

"I did everything you said; it didn't work." It happens. There's a lot to take into the journeying process, which is why I recommend taking it slow, build in small steps, and draw heavily on personal rituals and fetishes to support the process. That said, there are other factors that help or hinder how we glide between worlds. I've encountered six primary reasons that newcomers have problems journeying, and that veteran spiritwalkers sometimes reach an impasse. The following elaborates on those sticky spots, and troubleshoots moving through them:

Prescribing the senses
For most of us, journeying is intensely visual, though it doesn't have to be. Some people experience waking more through other senses, which is a fitting approach to exploring the spirit realms. If we perceive waking better another way, chances are that other way is a good place to start, regarding journeying. Despite the prevalent emphasis on 'seeing,' go with the sense that best suits you.

Likewise, be open to the possibilities. Just as we go to the other worlds to meet spirit allies, we also go there to meet other aspects of ourselves. For some of us those other aspects are senses, ways of perceiving that we haven't encountered before. Students often return from beginning journeys saying, "Nothing happened." What they really mean is, "Something happened, but I don't value it," as once we discuss their journey, without fail they express a shift in their awareness. Because it wasn't the shift they wanted or expected to experience, they didn't count it as journeying.

Sometimes it isn't the great hulking elephant waiting to greet us at the entry to our Lower World, but the crisp breeze, aroma of jasmine, song of birds, or resonant hoof beats. Perhaps it's even less tactile and is the sense of weightlessness, or an awareness of a presence. One way to practice opening to the senses in journey is to do so in waking. Most often, a magickal skill doesn't suddenly blossom in journey. Rather, through cultivation of how we perceive our waking, that ability is brought through and refined when we journey. In short, if we don't trust our perceptions in waking, we're not likely to trust them in trance. When we bless our waking experience, the other worlds give up lavish detail.

To address this, I encourage students to find a quiet, safe spot in Nature, of which they are very familiar. Set a timer for ten minutes, then get comfortable, and close or cover your eyes. Observe with every sense available the immediate surrounding area. You don't have to decode or give meaning to observations, just feel them through the duration of the exercise. If you want to apply meaning to them after, you may, though the focus is to observe and be present.

When you're comfortable with this practice, repeat it in a safe yet unfamiliar place. For kicks, try it with your ears plugged. If you really want to test your ability to be present and observe, blot the senses as much as possible and see what others emerge. The more you can widen your awareness to other senses, the more grounded you will be in the journey experience.

Presenting a poor intention
Another biggie for why journeying doesn't yield meaningful results is presenting the intention poorly. Wording matters. How we articulate the intention has everything to do with recognizing when it's been fulfilled. If we don't understand what we want to know, we won't recognize when insight has been given. Most often students present their intention as a question, the phrasing of which frequently leads to fruitless wandering. A clearly worded statement is best.

Sometimes despite a clear statement, the intention still

doesn't strike at the heart of what is most needed. For instance, I've had students present an intention such as, "I want to understand the history of heart disease in my family." It's a profound intention, and while it isn't wrong, it's limiting. Revised wording that cuts to the heart is, "I allow my guides to take me to the source of my family's history with heart disease." Not terribly different, the focus isn't on understanding the history, it's on engaging it, which can go in any direction. By opening how we're willing to perceive this source, we have allowed it infinite options in presenting itself to us.

Likewise, another example that I've seen often is, "I want to know my life purpose." Again, it's not bad phrasing, it's just not likely to impart the information we really want to know, which is how it feels to be living our life purpose. If we can feel that purpose, then we can not only know it, but recreate it anytime we want. It becomes neural memory. Thus, a more poignant intention may be, "I allow my guides to give me the experience of my life purpose," or, "I allow my guides to show me how it feels to live my life purpose."

Self-doubt
It plagues the best of us, and can strike at any point along the journey path. Most of us weren't raised to have faith in our own experiences, those of tactile five-sense origin, or ones of a more metaphoric, figurative significance.

Culturally, we've been conditioned to distrust our imaginations and not consider them contributors of meaningful data. As a result, we struggle to accept trance experiences as relevant. We can't easily get past questioning whether we saw or heard what we did. Unable to accept our observations, the journey experience can't unfold; thus, intentions for soul healing cannot be fulfilled. A complicating factor in self-doubt is that we don't expect to experience it. With that realization, shame looms large.

Resolution of self-doubt in journeying usually relies on

altering factors in the perception of self in formed reality, so that relaxation into the trance experience and affirmation of it can occur. Common proclamations of self-doubt that I hear regarding journeying are, "Nothing happened," or "I think I saw/heard/felt something, but I'm not sure." Each time one of these has come up, when I work back through the journey experience, what I find isn't that 'nothing happened.' Rather something did happen, but it was dismissed due to a lack of faith in personal perception. The observation was so small that it wasn't valued.

To release self-doubt, I support students in accepting their every intuitive impression. I challenge them to accept every perception as fact, no matter how surreal or far-fetched. If the sky is suddenly purple with yellow polka dots, I encourage them to accept for that moment, it was exactly as it appeared. If a second later, the same sky is cerulean blue with fluffy white clouds, honor it as such, and move on. No analysis required; just honor the observation and move on. Through encouraging them to realize that both perceptions are true and unrelated to each other, the need to compare or judge either perception is relinquished. Freedom from judging the perception allows the journey experience to unfold more freely.

Intuition requires confidence. When the need to judge observation is released, journeying can be accepted as another way to experience awareness. In blessing all observations, the emphasis isn't on accepting all data as fact, but on processing all perception as real. The empowerment of accepting all of our experiences as real opens pathways in journeying we would otherwise never find.

Lack of imagination
That sounds kind of harsh, doesn't it? Bear with me. Often, limitations in journeying are the result of limited awareness. What we can't conceive can't be. To draw on a contemporary

energy medicine teaching, life force follows awareness. What we put our attention on leads us forward. It allows us to fulfill our intention for journeying. However, some people don't have strong creative problem-solving skills, a requirement for meeting ecstatic intentions successfully. They may be entirely confident in their observations, but they don't know what to do with them, how to move them forward in a way that fulfills the intention. Sometimes called 'negotiation' by traditional shamans, unleashing boundless, rollicking imagination not only ensures meeting obligations in the journey space, but solidifies the personal experience of it. Imagination is needed in journeying not just for navigation, but for interaction with the spirits of the worlds, themselves.

The most overt place I've found a lack of imagination to be a hindrance is in finding the way around the spirit realms. The lack of sign posts pointing us along can be disconcerting, as is finding a legend unlike what was expected. What if the road just ends? What if there is no road? What if a totem isn't forthcoming with information? How, then, can the journey proceed?

When students feel constricted in their imaginations, I direct them to call in their five-year-old superhero personas. Many adults are uncomfortable reaching back into the limitless imaginations of their youth, seeing that untamed logic as archaic, erratic, or invaluable. The truth is, that wild mind can solve anything, because it knows no bounds. This primal youth knows how to ask for directions from a bird. It understands that when the road dead-ends, it's okay to weave between the grasses. It rests comfortably jumping off a cliff to soar higher.

When we can realize that every facet of the spirit world is alive and responsive, we begin crafting our unique dialogue. Yes, the ability to intuitively read and navigate the events and symbols of the spirit realm meets our needs for the journey. It also sets the stage for how future journeys unfold. Ecstatic trance is a dialogue that builds with every adventure. Forming this fluid relationship with the mechanism of journeying is the core of the ecstatic practice. This merging of the imagination with the spirit world teaches us how to decipher personal signals. It enables us to form relationships with guides, scapes, elements, forces, absolutely everything in the journey space. These relationships are what shape the shaman.

Over-rationalization

One of the most valuable skills of the modern mind is the ability to rationalize observations, information, and experience. In truth, there is great need for rationale in spirit travel, as it provides us the necessary anchor to know when we are pushing beyond our boundaries, to know when we're venturing too far into our unknown and need to retreat. Originating from the protective ego, reason fosters our sense of control, mitigates negotiation and compromise, and governs self-importance. Each of these attributes brings stability to ecstatic trance, though when over-developed causes it to stall.

Confronted with students who over-rationalize their journey experiences, questions that most frequently arise are: "Is it real?" "Am I making it up?" "What if I only see what I want to see?" "What if it's just my imagination?" These are all very logical and responsible inquiries that I encourage as healthy self-checks of trance students. Assessment of the journey experience allows us to derive meaning from our observations and our feelings about them. The ability to hold our impressions in this way can shed greater light in how they facilitate meeting our intention for the journey.

However, when the scrutiny doesn't stop at gentle prodding and progresses to over-rationalization of trance, the intended soul work can't be completed. To those who become stunted in a loop of recursive logic, I pose these questions: "Is it real compared to what?" "Are you making this up from what?" "What do you want to see?" "What if it is just your imagination?

Is your imagination real? Can you accept that the spirit realms are real if you believe your imagination is fake? Are your dreams fake?" The bottom line is, if you can control what is occurring in the journey, you're not in trance. If you attempt to control the journey and it has other plans for you, you're in. You're doing it.

Perhaps devoting some thought to defining what is real would help. Often when we deeply examine what "real" means, we conclude how little value such a measure has, not just in ecstasy, but perhaps throughout life. Likewise, ascertaining that what we make up has as much value as something we don't make up, or as something someone else makes up, releases self-judgment regarding the observation.

For those who don't have clarity on their expectations of journeying, I have them think of something they want to occur in the trance. When I facilitate them to engage with the desired occurrence, without fail the interaction and dialogue is unexpected. We can't predict what our guides will do, suggest, or say. That is what distinguishes this kind of trance from meditation and guided visualization. For the purpose of shamanic work, we may be in the driver's seat, but we're not the GPS. We will it otherwise. Through understanding this distinction, journeying becomes the difference between plotting a course and being led. We become open to what is, instead of what we think should be.

The core of over-rationalizing ecstatic trance events lies in realizing that what we have often asserted as beliefs are most often assumptions. Journeying challenges assumptions we've made about how we perceive reality and ourselves in it. When soulful interaction holds meaning for us, it becomes intuition. When we feel that personal truth, it is real. The need to question is becomes moot.

Unwanted outcome

In that freedom of being the driver though not the GPS,

sometimes things don't go the way we'd like. As inebriating as the distance created by over-analyzing whether we created a journey experience is the shock of realizing we didn't. Entering into the finer workings of ecstatic trance plays havoc with our habit of setting expectations. Whether we mean to or through no conscious effort of our own, when we attune to the mastery of soul travel, we bring with us certain expectations of the flight and its results. That said, sometimes we see things we aren't prepared to see. Such revelations can blind-side so thoroughly that we're left questioning the role of journeying, if not shamanism, in our lives.

Most of us expect that sacred trip to be smooth and captivating, validating us in some way. While the journey experience is intensely riveting, on occasion it's profound through sobering, if not staggering, revelations. Harkening to our cultural lack of an animistic worldview, often fledgling journeys give a first glimpse into how that hunger has shaped our spiritual lives. An otherwise blissful experience of homecoming into the spiritual manifestation of ourselves, into acceptance and full realization of self, can be extremely stressful, certainly traumatic. As well, some students new to the practice embark on journeying and are met with known wounds that need deeper tending, or discover hurts they hadn't sourced, prior. A joyful meeting with a deceased loved one can change perception of life in such a way that while the journey was lovely, how one returns to carry that experience forward can create an emotional dilemma. Others meet a facet of self who demands radical change in waking life, adamant expression in an unsupportive community.

While each of these possibilities offers vast opportunity for healing and growth, they present intense spiritual crises that must be resolved to master shamanic journeying. For some students these crisis overwhelm the desire to journey, and they abandon it as a spiritual practice.

For these unwanted outcomes, grounding around the journey

experience is required. Ideally, all of the preparatory work for journeying hasn't just been studied, but mastered, as we mentioned in earlier chapters—crafting rituals, fetishes, discussion about the ley of the soulscape and all that it may serve up. Having a firm relationship with these before experiential exploration can make all the difference in what happens during and after. As well, skills in mindfulness and emotional release should be identified, honed. Support systems should be noted and made actively on call. A compassionate, knowledgeable mentor should be part of the ecstatic education. Through greater mundane awareness, when unwanted outcomes arise in journey, a plan is already in place to foster and midwife those experiences and feelings to assimilate them into wisdom.

For students who encounter unwanted outcomes in journey, I facilitate them back into trance right away. Such crises become initiations, that unaddressed create spiritual post-traumatic stress, or soul loss. The sooner they can be confronted and healed, the more solidly journey can be approached again.

Considering the challenges of shamanic journeying for modern seekers, while its mechanics can be learned in a weekend class, developing the compass for how to do so cannot. Mastery of ecstatic trance isn't just about refining the ability to journey, but to know what to do with the spoils of spirit travel. My best advice remains find a mentor who can give context, thus support the ongoing destination. And of course, practice, practice, practice.

Tips for ecstatic journeying
- Restate your intention if you find nothing is happening or feel unfocused.
- Ask your totem to move you to your destination, or the next significant place along your destination.
- If needed, call in a totem specifically for assisting in spirit travel, and do what it says.

- Refocus on the drum, should your focus meander.
- Refocus on your breath (inhale, draw in the belly, exhale expand the belly).
- Always retrace your steps upon leaving.
- Explore one intention at a time. There's a tendency to tack on details. Don't bog down what you really need to know.
- By the same token, once you've received what you need, leave. Begin backtracking. When you belabor the journey, it begins to lose power. You start to lose the thread of your intention, thus forget the wisdom you've gained.

Service to Community

We've talked in-depth about the roots of shamanism and the ground they've covered in modern spirituality. What a shaman does and how it's done we've explored from different vantage points. Around this juncture in studying shamanism, a specific crossroads is met, which is discerning personal need on a shamanic path from taking on the role of shaman. A key distinction between shamanism as a personal path and acting as a spiritual conduit on the behalf of others is in the servitude to community. This component also further distinguishes shamanism from other intuitive paths.

An often overlooked component of modern shamanism is paying service to a specific community. Historically shamans served their tribes. Traditional shamans are born into their communities, so they don't have to soul search to find one. They come into the world with the support system to witness, honor, bless, and grow their wild, intuitive selves from day one. Such is not so evident in the West.

Until recent emphasis on ecodynamics entered contemporary pagan consciousness, modern shamanism largely has been presented and implemented as a personal exercise in spiritual growth, self-healing. As we discussed in earlier chapters, this drive to heal at a spiritual level could be the contemporary equivalent of the classic shamanic death, the spiritual crisis that calls to action. For many modern seekers, the path stops at the personal healing level. It doesn't blossom into servitude. Certainly healing the self benefits all, though this focus indicates an animistic perspective more so than a shamanic one. In the wider arena of shamanism, one who doesn't serve a community is not considered a shaman. Practicing shamanic technique isn't definitive. Rather, the emphasis of shamanism is to be a spiritual conduit between the community and the Divine.

This is a deeply personal choice. I encourage students to come to their own conclusions about wearing the mantle of shaman, and clarifying where self-healing and working with others fits into that. For me, such is the distinction between a mystic and a shaman. Mystics may work with others, though their focus stays mostly on the cultivation of their personal path and wellbeing. Shamans take that focus to the next level by leading, representing, working in, and growing a community. They commit not only to facilitating its present wellbeing, but to actively, if not publicly, supporting its ability to thrive, ever more.

Perhaps serving a community is the desired path, though there is uncertainty about what community to engage. Knowing right away isn't a requirement. In fact, even when it seems very clear, I encourage sitting with that insight a bit to see what other truths clarify. Given that my inroad for personal shamanic healing revolved around sexual abuse in my childhood, I fully expected my formation of community to comprise some facet of working with assault survivors. However, no matter how much I devoted to that work, I was pulled to mentoring intuitives experiencing spiritual emergence. No matter how I put out the intention for working with survivors to be my community, the clients and students who darkened my doorway were budding seers and healers, every day people reeling from some experience of the wyrd that left them wholly changed and oppressively alone in their transition. Most of them were survivors, though their crisis at present revolved around a lack of support for their spiritual awakening.

But I didn't want that to be my community. I didn't want to walk back through my rootless beginnings as an intuitive. Doing so would force me to recall decades of knowing I was different in a way that defied vocabulary, the endless frustration and depression around feeling called to something that had no boundaries or guidelines, the loneliness of a solitary path, and the fear of many inexplicable phenomena that were part of my norm. I didn't want to revisit any of those things or the feelings they stirred. Yet in greeting the stories of others, mine re-emerged as a strong shamanic narrative, encouraging others to stay the course and affirming that they weren't alone. Along with reviewing my history of spiritual emergency came unexpected emotional snarls tangling my abusive childhood once again with my spiritual path, even if only that both were occurring at the same time, that despite trauma from those different sources, the pain felt the same.

Most of the clients who came to me for this support never spoke of the supernatural events in their lives to anyone but me. They entrusted me with their most precious secrets. How in the world would I create community when we had all been so ostracized in our personal lives that we couldn't even speak our truths unless we thought only the Divine was listening?

I've been on my healing path since I was six years old. From the age of seventeen I began my shamanic path. At twenty-seven I began working with others as a facilitator of healing. I realize now, as with all spiritual truths, the shaman doesn't find the community, the community finds the shaman.

Keep in mind that "community" can be defined many ways. For some, community is a group of people sharing a common geographic location, working diligently with all life that falls under that bioregional scope. For others, community is a specific forest, working with a particular type of suffering spirit, or working with a group managing certain life experiences or issues.

However this concept of unity speaks, if shamanism is the desired path, it will eventually speak. Remember that everything is alive. Do a Middle World journey, inviting the spirit of the community that needs you to come, speak, engage. By greeting this spirit at the deepest levels, its physical manifestation can come more gently into being.

What do you think?

Begin assessing what role shamanism fills for you on a personal and community level. How do you define community? Consider what community needs you to act as a conduit with the Divine.

What are your thoughts on wounding and its connection to initiation into shamanhood? What purpose might overcoming personal struggle serve in the creation of a shaman? Should every shaman have to go through this process?

Ethics

As we've covered the intangible details of shamanism, like setting boundaries, calling on guides for help, and creating relationships to support us along our growth, a logical progression in that dialogue is the topic of ethics. Even if the plan is to maintain shamanism as only a personal path and not work with others, the discussion of ethics remains relevant. However you approach shamanism, creating a code of conduct for working with self, spirit allies, Nature, and eventually others is important.

Ethics is generally defined as a guideline delineating right and wrong, as applicable to a specific implementation, circumstance, or group. As an animist, having a sense of ethics isn't just about honoring guidelines, but also honoring the spirit from which they were created. Sometimes referred to as "moral principles," perhaps a sense of ethics has already come from trance work or other spiritual practice. We do bring into our spiritual boundaries other aspects of our lives, as how we interact with diverse people can deeply inform us in how to engage spirits. I advise students at minimum to come to an understanding of what spiritual practices are healthy and supportive and those that are not, what acquisition of ritual tools supports humane and sustainable life and that which does not, and accountability in the shaman-Spirit Guide relationship. In the latter criterion I include helping spirits, totems, scapes, and elements. If it's a consciousness that informs us, we must uphold our end of that relationship in some way.

A very fuzzy area, ethics, the intent of this discussion isn't to prescribe what it should be; rather, to present common criteria of ethics in a spiritual practice, so that we can each form our own code. In that light, here is a list of considerations for creating a personal ethical code, paired with examples of each:

- Right and wrong spiritual practices (closing sacred space, cultural appropriation)

- Healthy lifestyle observances (journeying when exhausted or sick, caring for body and mind as thoroughly as soul)
- Humane and sustainable use of animal/plant/land material in ritual (compassionate acquisition of fetishes, reseeding used plants)
- Criticism of spiritual path (how to take it, respect others' unverified personal gnosis (UPG))
- Use of intuition for positive purposes (heal others only with permission, keep cosmic hands to self)
- Shared spiritual space (skyclad rituals, maintaining personal sacred space in a group)
- Merging waking ethics with those of ecstasy (bioregional responsibility, social accountability)
- Paying it forward with guides/totems (monthly wildlife volunteer, pick up litter campaign, feed the homeless)
- Accountability to land spirits (involvement in local community issues, participation in functions)

What do you think?

If you intend to keep shamanism as only a personal path, what ethics are important to you in treatment of yourself? Of your helping spirits? Of Nature, and the resources you use to support your spiritual growth?

List your spirit helpers and the resources you use most in your rituals and journeys. What is right use of them? What constitutes poor or abusive use of them? How might you need to change your lifestyle to support your spiritual code of ethics?

If you intend to engage others in your spiritual path, what guidelines are most important to you? What boundaries do you need them to honor regarding your spirituality, space, person, methods? What boundaries should you honor of others?

How do you honor the land?

What makes you accountable?

As you develop your code of ethics, invoke its spirit, and engage it in deciding what conduct should be addressed.

Legalities

Some aspects of shamanism warrant impeccable understanding of local and national legalities regarding freedom of religion, the use of entheogens in spiritual ceremony, and possession of ritual items such as feathers, animal skins, or parts. Working with such tools isn't required to create, shape, and maintain an evolving shamanic path. However, it's important to have a clear understanding of how psychoactive plants and the ritual use of animal parts is viewed in your region.

For instance, many people don't realize that while it grows wild around the world, *Salvia Divinorum* is illegal in some states and countries. Growing it, let alone using it, can come with legal repercussions. Likewise, in the United States, many feathers—even commonly found ones such as barn owl and hawk—are illegal in the possession of those who are not Native American, even for spiritual use. As well, in many cases due to the fragile existence of some animal species, working with even found (as in, not purchased or ones you hunted) animal parts is illegal. Contact a local game or wildlife agency to determine the specifications for working with plants and animal parts.

Does this make me Pagan?

A question that comes up invariably from students new on the shamanic path is whether this work makes them Pagan. Well, yes, unless it doesn't. In truth, every major world religion at one point had a mystical tradition that encompassed animistic observations, shamanistic practices. From the Hindu faith came the practice of Yoga. Christianity hosted then departed from Gnosticism. Judaism shrouded esoteric secrets in the Kabbalah, while Islam experienced enlightenment via Sufism. Of all of these religions, only Hinduism never segregated its mystical roots.

From the standpoint that shamanism is rooted in the animistic belief that all things have a soul, all souls are connected, all souls can intercommunicate via that connection, and all souls are equal... it's a Pagan practice. This doesn't necessarily mean that one's birth religion has to go the wayside. I know many Christians who implement shamanistic approaches and perspectives into an eclectic, yet Christ-centric faith. It is important to understand that earth-based mystical practices are considered pagan, and that we all reserve the right to refer to ourselves however we prefer.

However identified, others may and likely will bring biases in their perception of the shamanic path. Consider how to handle that. I've worked with people from many walks of life—ethnicities, orientations, nationalities, religions, cultures, economic statuses. Regardless of what brought them to me or their thought on what I do, every one of them had an experience that challenged their current belief system or life experience in a way they felt could only be addressed spiritually. That was the one common bond, and it's enough to do a lot of wonderful work.

Likewise, I interact with many people fascinated with what I do, yet we don't work together. The common factor with this group is an experience of the paranormal that fell outside their religious and sometimes even scientific explanation. Everybody has a spooky story.

While these ways of connecting may not resonate for everyone, find what will. As we interact with more people in the shamanic community and reveal shamanism to our social circles as part of our path, identify where they find common ground, and affirm it.

How do I tell my parents?

It's never easy telling your parents things they may not want to hear, harder still to explain to them something important to you that they don't understand. First off, check out some great books on the topic:

- *DIY Totemism* by Lupa
- *New Paths to Animal Totems* by Lupa
- *Traveling Between the Worlds* by Hillary S. Webb
- *Exploring Shamanism* by Hillary S. Webb
- *Kids Who See Ghosts* by Caron Goode
- *Shamanic Journeying: A Beginner's Guide* by Sandra Ingerman
- *Shaman, Healer, Sage* by Alberto Villoldo
- *Awakening to the Spirit World* by Sandra Ingerman and Hank Wesselman

Sometimes giving others the option of educating themselves on a topic goes further than explaining it in the context of your own life. Allowing them to grasp broad components of shamanism in a general context can give ample room to digest what's currently captivating the attention of their darling child.

Still, a book can't substitute for the fact that you want them to understand shamanism is at least a personal interest, if not a life path for you. Much like finding like-minded others in mixed neopagan forums, with your family, focus on the commonalities, rather than the differences. Find the places where your paths share similarities, such as Spirit Guides and angels, the concept of the Divine, sacred experiences in Nature, and the concept of Sacred Space.

Don't:

React angrily. It's okay to express frustration in not feeling supported by them. However, expressing feeling unsupported is more likely to keep communication open with them than ranting or lashing out.

Criticize their spiritual path. Shamanism works for you. It may not for others. There is no right or wrong. Part of their ability to accept you on your path is your acceptance of them on theirs.

Offer to journey for them. You're too new to this process to cross those kinds of personal streams with your parents. Most shamans don't do journey work with close loved ones.

Get upset if their response isn't what you want it to be. From their perspective, you aren't just changing your personal spiritual path, but are removing a common tie they've likely always shared with you. From their perception, this is a loss of a joint community, social circle, and holiday traditions. In many ways they fear they're losing their baby. Honor their response, and address their fears with understanding and affirmation of your presence in their lives.

Do:

Have realistic expectations. You know how your parents are likely to react to learning of your spiritual interests. Be honest with yourself, and prepare for their reaction. Allow their reaction.

Get their attention. Don't drop your spiritual interests on your parents in the middle of a public event, a stressful time, or when they're otherwise distracted. You and they deserve full focus on each other. Talk with them at a mutually agreeable time. Schedule it, if necessary.

Think about what you're going to say to them, ahead of time. Write it down if it helps. Practice explaining to them your interest in shamanism and what it means to you, and prepare to provide a lot of references.

Give them room not to take you seriously. After all, you used to dress yourself in purple pants and an orange polka-dotted shirt, and went through how many instruments/sports/subjects until you found one that held your interest long-term? Parents have a hard time letting go of the perception that their children can't fend for themselves or stay with interests over time.

Allow them space to process. Don't expect them to leap to support you right away. If they do, bless it. If not, consider how you can continue on your path, yet honor their space to take it all in, at the same time.

Allow them to ask you questions. Most loved ones just don't understand shamanism. They either hold the same biases we've discussed in this book, or know nothing at all about its origins or use. Indulge their curiosity, though don't present yourself as your own authority by knowing the answers. Suggest books I've listed for them to educate themselves.

Ask them to share their concerns. At the end of it all, their trepidation about having their child on a different spiritual path comes down to concern for your welfare. Give them a chance to voice their feelings and be prepared to honor them. Allay fears by being knowledgeable and giving them straight answers.

Respect them. The key thing you will face on a shamanic path is others not understanding what you do, and some not caring to understand. The reaction of your parents may be your first opportunity to practice the respect you seek.

Tell them you love them. As you need to retain their affection, they need yours, as well. And you need them to know that because your spiritual path has changed doesn't mean your feelings for them have.

Discuss plans to find a mentor. Most likely your mentor will want your parents included in your study plans. In fact, your parents' knowledge will likely be required. Include them in the process of finding and greeting a mentor, if possible.

Where to learn more

At best, this book is a survey, a primer in the many directions available on the path of the modern shaman. There are many opportunities to learn more in literature, on websites, and from shamanic practitioners around the world. If you would like to locate a modern shaman near you and can't find someone reputable to work with, feel free to contact me for a reference. I am happy to share resources with shamans from all over the world and with seekers, alike.

Organizations and Resources

Aviela, Inc. – www.malidoma.com

Contemporary Shaman – www.contemporaryshaman.net

Irish Centre for Shamanic Studies –
www.shamanismireland.com

Riverdrum – www.riverdrum.com

Shaman Portal – www.shamanportal.org

Shamanic Teachers – www.shamanicteachers.com

Shamanism Canada – www.shamanismcanada.com

Shared Wisdom – www.sharedwisdom.com

Society of Shamanic Practitioners – www.shamansociety.org

Soul Intent Arts – www.soulintentarts.com

The Foundation for Shamanic Studies – www.shamanism.org

The Four Winds Society – www.thefourwinds.com

The Green Wolf – www.thegreenwolf.com

The Last Mask Center – www.lastmaskcenter.org

The Sacred Trust – www.sacredtrust.org

Walking Stick Foundation – www.walkingstick.org

About the Author

Kelley is a modern shaman and author in North Carolina. A lifelong intuitive, she has been on a shamanic path since 1988, and since 2000 has served her local community and an international client base through Soul Intent Arts. Her memoir, *Gift of the Dreamtime – Awakening to the Divinity of Trauma*, chronicles her pivotal step from spiritual crisis into shamanism. *Real Wyrd – A Modern Shaman's Roots in the Middle World* is a collection of essays on supernatural experiences throughout her life. She publishes *The Weekly Rune* cast on *The Huffington Post*, and since 2004 has maintained the blog, *Intentional Insights: Q&A From Within*, addressing reader inquiries on animism, shamanism, and the everyday paranormal. On *PaganSquare* she writes about spiritual life in postmodern suburbia, in the feature *The Isolated Animist*.

Through her shamanic practice she has established the *Tribe of the Modern Mystic*, bringing international support and mentorship to individuals as they grow into powerful abilities, and providing shamanic community support for personal spiritual emergence. Her practice comprises in-person and distance healing sessions, classes, Mystery School, mentoring, and ceremonial artistry in the community.

Learn more about Kelley's work at:
www.soulintentarts.com.
Follow her at:
www.facebook.com/s.kelleyharrell, @skelleyh.
Follow Soul Intent Arts at:
www.facebook.com/soulintentarts, @soulintentarts.

References

1   If you're interested in reading more about these experiences, I recount some of the stories in my books: *Exploring Shamanism, Traveling between the Worlds,* and *Yanantin and Masintin in the Andean World.*

2   From *Traveling Between the Worlds: Conversations with Contemporary Shamans* (p. 11) by Hillary S. Webb.

3   Ripinsky-Naxon, Michael, *The Nature of Shamanism: Substance and Function of a Religious Metaphor* (New York, State University of New York Press, 1993)

4   Max Dashu, http://www.suppressedhistories.net/articles/womanshaman.html

5   Tedlock, Barbara, The Woman in the Shaman's Body: Reclaiming the Feminine in Religion and Medicine (Bantam, 2005).

6   Harper, Douglas, *Online Etymology Dictionary,* http://www.etymonline.com/index.php?term=shaman

7   Kehoe, Alice, *Shamans and Religion: An Anthropological Exploration in Critical Thinking,* (Illinois: Waveland Press, Inc., 2000)

8   Grof, Stanislav Grof. *Spiritual Emergency: When Personal Transformation Becomes a Crisis,* Tarcher, 1989.

9   Farmer, Steven D. Sacred *Ceremony – How to Create Ceremonies for Healing, Transitions, and Celebrations.* Hay House, 2002.

10 Webb, Hillary S. *Traveling Between the Worlds – Conversations with Contemporary Shamans.* Hampton Roads Publishing Company, Inc., 2004.

11 Elert, Glenn. *Frequency of Brain Waves,* from *The Physics Factbook*™. http://hypertextbook.com/facts/2004/Samantha Charles.shtml

12 http://en.wikipedia.org/wiki/Totemism

13   Andrews, Ted. *Animal Speak – The Spiritual and Magical Powers of Creatures Great and Small.* Llewellyn Publications, 1993.

Soul Rocks is a fresh list that takes the search for soul and spirit mainstream. Chick-lit, young adult, cult, fashionable fiction & non-fiction with a fierce twist.